# Stronger Than Death

# Stronger Than Death

## Sue Chance, M.D.

W · W · NORTON & COMPANY · *NEW YORK* · *LONDON*

FIRST EDITION

The text of this book is composed in Avanta and the display type is set in Centaur
and Eterna. Manufacturing is by The Haddon Craftsmen. Book design by Marjorie J.
Flock.

Library of Congress Cataloging–in–Publication Data

Chance, Sue.
    Stronger than death / Sue Chance.
        p.    cm.
    Includes bibliographical references and index.
    1. Suicide—Psychological aspects.   2. Bereavement—Psychological aspects.   3. Suicide
victims—Family relationships.   I. Title. HV6545.C43   1992
362.2′8—dc20

ISBN 0-393-03092-X

W.W. Norton & Company, Inc., 500 Fifth Avenue, New York, N.Y. 10110
W.W. Norton & Company Ltd., 10 Coptic Street, London WC1A 1PU

1 2 3 4 5 6 7 8 9 0

# Contents

# Stronger Than Death

In our sleep, Pain that cannot forget
Falls drop by drop upon the Heart
And in our Despair, against our Will
Comes Wisdom through the awful grace of God.

— AESCHYLUS

HE WAS ALWAYS CONSIDERATE—even in the way he blew out his brains.

He started his note, "I love you all," and made it clear that nobody was to blame but him.

He left the house after everyone was asleep, drove to a park just outside town, parked his pickup in a conspicuous place, sat on the riverbank and drank a six-pack as fast as he could, then stretched out full length, put the .38 Derringer to his left temple, and pulled the trigger.

The blast that ended his life started a shitstorm for his family.

November 16, 1984

# Tidings of Great Pain

SOMETIMES, I JUST PUTZ AROUND—especially on Fridays. It's usually a half-day for me, so I tell myself it doesn't matter *which* four hours I work, just so I get in my four hours. Of course, being a doctor, I may work more or less than that (usually more), but four's the built-in number my pacer comes up with when I open my eyes and languorously stretch. O Glorious Friday.

That particular one, I decided that I needed a pair of shoes to go with my new navy suit. Since the mall didn't open until ten, I took my time, lying in bed awhile, then having several cups of coffee. Once I'd bought the shoes and done a little more shopping, I decided to pick up some food and have lunch with my husband, Tom, before going to the hospital.

I'd been in a fairly good mood, but as we ate, I grew quieter and, in one of those empathic moments married couples have, Tom held out his arms to me. I moved over to sit on his lap and he asked me what was wrong. I was suddenly on the verge of tears, without a clue as to why and, after several moments, I answered, "I don't know. Maybe I just need a week at a fat farm."

He chuckled and said, "No, you don't."

I hugged him tighter, unable to come up with an explanation for why I felt as I did.

We sat like that for several minutes. Then the phone rang. It was Carla, one of the secretaries in the clinic where I worked and, in what I thought was an odd voice, she told me Ken, the psychiatrist who owned the clinic, needed to speak with me before I went to the hospital. Thinking he'd probably forgotten to do something for one of his patients that morning, I said okay, I'd stop by in about half an hour.

When I got to the office, Carla looked upset as I walked by, pointing to Ken's office and asking, "He in there?" She nodded without looking up and, if I thought anything at all, it was that she would tell me what was wrong if it had to do with me; otherwise, her feelings were her business. That's the biggest misunderstanding people have about psychiatrists, that we are always analyzing the people around us. Actually, we're more than glad to allow others their privacy. Figuring people out takes too much time and attention to do it frivolously.

Ken closed the door. An alarm sounded very distantly but, since I was in Ken's reassuring company and have this innocent illusion that nothing bad happens to us when we're around good people, I ignored it. Then he sat down in his swivel chair and turned toward me, face on. It's hard to explain why that sounded another alarm. I suppose it's based on the observation that, the better two people know each other, the less conventional their conversational arrangements become. With strangers and in business, observing the forms is important—shaking hands, putting the other at ease, maintaining eye contact—all these are ways of establishing good intentions. With friends and family, our good intentions are assumed, so we toss words over our shoulder while sorting the pile on our desk. Ken's facing me as he did was a breach of that less formal etiquette.

His words are a blur, the sheer weight of the message crushing their fragile memory. I know he broke it to me in stages—that my son had shot himself, that he had been found that morning, that he'd been in a park, that the news had come from my sister, who hadn't wanted to call me at home, fearing I might be alone. I only remember asking two questions. One was whether or not he was dead and the other was whether he'd done it by shooting himself in the head. I knew the answer to both. I suppose I asked to make it official and to see if there were some magical way to wriggle out of the awful reality.

How did I know that Jim had shot himself in the head? I knew it because I knew he'd *make sure.* My son was, like me, the irrevocable sort. For better or worse, a decision made is a fait accompli. I'm not saying that's good. I'm just saying it's part of the family genetic code.

When Ken told me the things he knew, he did a wonderful, human thing, a thing for which I will bless him the rest of my life. He gave me exactly what I needed, not too much, not too little. When the agony hit me, I doubled over, sobbing, "Oh God! Oh God!" And, knowing me—knowing that, although I want comforting, I need it on my terms—he moved his chair closer to me. He was close enough to touch if I gave any indication I wanted to be touched, but he left enough distance for my space to be my own. And, as I am prone to do, I chose to pull into myself, to plunge into that radiant core of pain alone.

Why?

Because I discovered long ago that we are alone in the important things. The moment we cleave from our mothers, we are alone. The moment we cleave from life, we are alone. If we connect with others in between, it is an act of will, and in moments of extremity I lack the will. I can't reach; I can only huddle. I bless Ken for knowing that and for not compounding my agony by offering something I couldn't accept, by adding awkwardness to that agony.

I said some practical things about calling my sister, Peggy, going home, taking time off. I think I carefully explained what my patients should and shouldn't be told. It wasn't necessary, of course. Not in any literal sense. Then, I went to my office, closed the door, sat down, got up, sat down, got up. I'm sure it worried Ken and Carla sick, but I wasn't thinking about them.

I cried very hard very briefly, then called Peggy. The only thing I remember saying was, "I feel so bad." Sounds innocuous, doesn't it? It meant a world of things. It meant I was overwhelmed with guilt and pain and devastation. It meant, "I can't live. There's no air." I think she told me it wasn't my fault. She knew I'd assume it was since I characteristically assume things are my fault.

I tried to call Tom, but it was his custom never to answer the phone since it was usually for me. I tried all kinds of signals, but nothing got him to pick it up. I felt like screaming, but instead I walked down the hall, said to a startled Ken and Carla, "I'm going home now. I can't get Tom." Both offered to drive me. I said very reasonably that it was too much trouble since it meant either leaving my car on the parking lot or one of them having to walk back to the clinic. I was out the door before they could tackle me. I know Ken protested. I also know I ignored him.

When I got home, Tom had put the chain on the door. It was perfectly reasonable, since the maintenance people in the apartment complex had a bad habit of sailing in with little warning. I nearly went berserk. I began to jerk the door repeatedly, growling with rage. I was just about to start kicking it and flinging myself against it when Tom got it open. Then, I carefully took several steps and sat my purse down in its usual place, turned to Tom, and said, "Jim killed himself." I started to say something else, but Tom's face contorted and he reached for me, saying, "Oh, God." And, I was finally able to release a cry of anguish which, this time, was a plea for help.

My husband picked me up, carried me up the stairs, then lay down, holding me while I screamed and sobbed. He didn't ask questions, didn't speak for a long time, but he held the fragments together, knowing I couldn't right then.

When he finally spoke, it was to tell me the truth. He said, "You're crying for *your* pain. Jim's is over."

It's taken me years to explore and partially understand that. I'll tell you everything I've discovered about it, but I want you to know up front that the quest may last as long as I do.

# TWO

# Going Home

JIM LIVED IN SAN ANGELO—which, for the uninitiated, is near the center of Texas, but is always referred to as "West Texas." With a population around 80,000, it isn't a small town. But then, it isn't a metropolis either. It's where I grew up, where Jim was born, and where my sister, parents, and several nieces still live.

I was living in Clear Lake, a suburb of Houston, when Jim died, and since there was no direct flight to San Angelo, we decided to fly into Midland, rent a car, and drive the remaining 150 miles.

That trip was an ordeal. I stayed chilled and kept my coat on the entire time, even though I was aware of several people staring at me, puzzled. I think they could tell I was a casualty; they just didn't know of what. And it wasn't that I was crying—I didn't do that until Tom and I were in the rental car. I think there must have been a kind of stunned aura around me because I remember people speaking a little more softly, being a little less pushy.

In the car, Tom either let me talk and cry without commenting or he stroked my back or pulled me against him. God bless him. Touching beats out words at a time like that. People always groan, "I don't know what to say." Fine. Don't talk. If you know the bereaved well enough to feel pity, then touch them. That's what they need, since the sound of a rending heart drowns out all words.

When we got there, my father had gone to bed. My sister, brother, sister-in-law, and mother were waiting, but not long after we got there, my mother went to bed also.

Therein lies a tale. . . .

It would take a very long time to straighten out the chronology, all the whys and wherefores, but Jim had lived with my parents (except for the year he was thirteen) since he was eleven. His first year with them, I lived there too, since I had recently divorced and was finishing my last year of college. You might say that I was an early bloomer in some respects and a late one in others—meaning that I married at fifteen, had my son at seventeen, graduated from college at twenty-nine, from medical school at thirty-six, and from residency at forty-one. Science calls that a "bimodal distribution"—meaning that, if you stacked up big events under a curve, my life curve would look like a camel's back—two peaks with a sag in between. That's sort of how it was, now that I come to think of it.

I don't know what Jim's life curve looked like to him. To me, it was a fairly flat line. From the time he was eleven or twelve, he worked either part or full time as a welder for my father. That continued through high school and during the years he sporadically went to college. When he died at age twenty-five, he had about three years of college credits, since he had taken semesters off here and there because of chronic back pain or tendonitis of his wrist.

On one level they puzzled me, his persistent health problems. On another, they made perfect sense. Pain is often a metaphor for pain, and we express our psychological difficulties through that most available mode of expression, our body. But after Jim got past the colic and teething and runny noses of his babyhood, he was a robust, energetic little guy who easily ran on less sleep than I did. Looking back, I don't think he'd have qualified for a diagnosis of hyperactivity, but he was definitely geared higher than his Mom. And his restlessness was a family joke. Some part of him was ever in motion—feet tapping, fingers drumming, eyes darting—he seemed to dance through a room. A corollary joke was the way he'd disappear. Nobody ever knew how long they'd be talking to him. Pause and he might vanish. Jim did not *do* lulls.

Green eyes with brown flecks. I can close my eyes this moment and see them as clearly as though it were seven minutes ago—instead of the seven years it's been. I last saw him the Christmas before he died. Christmas of 1983. The last real Christmas for me.

I scratched his head. I never had before. I did it absent-mindedly, since he was sitting on the floor near my chair and I'd gotten in the habit of scratching my husband's head. When I realized what I was doing, I grew flustered and started to withdraw my hand. Jim put his hand up, holding mine in his hair while he laughed and said, "No, I like it. Feel free."

I never thought about it then, but touching Jim was almost always on his terms. Hugs were okay, but kisses were very dicey. I was startled when I went through pictures later and found the same old composition, regardless of who was with him. In picture after picture, the person who loves Jim is standing with an arm around him. His hands are either in his pockets or tucked into his armpits.

Our children only *seem* known to us. That's because we equate knowledge of events and habits with comprehension. We were there when they came into being so we think we know what sort of people they are. We are totally blind to the fact that we can't know what they feel unless they tell us. Most of us know that about strangers. None of us knows that about our children. Few of us know it about spouses, parents, siblings, lovers, friends, co-workers, or patients.

Put that on your refrigerator door: YOU DON'T KNOW WHAT OTHERS FEEL UNLESS THEY TELL YOU. It's good to know in any circumstances. It's vital to know if you're a suicide survivor.

I lay there the night Jim died asking myself the question every survivor asks, "Why? Why, why, why, why, why?" Let me make sense of it so I can bear it. If I can only assemble an explanation, then I can see where I failed and correct it. Maybe that won't undo this, but it'll keep me from killing anybody else with my neglect or my insensitivity or my whatever-the-hell-I-did-wrong. Better to be a monster with some hope for change than to be at the mercy of this malign randomness.

It's too hard to be a gnat, crushed by the thoughtless flick of some universal sacred cow's tail. Somebody tell me what I did. Go ahead—I can take it. As a matter of fact, I think Jim should tell me. Yes, that's right. Jim. He can come back and point a finger at me and tell me a long, long list of everything I did wrong so I can say I'm sorry and I'll do better if he'll just give me a chance. I *would* do better. I promise.

But, in the fitful two hours I slept that night, Jim only came back long enough to tell me he was okay and that I wasn't to worry and that *he* was sorry.

"I'm sorry, Mom," he said, his voice soft and gentle.

I pretended for both our sakes that it comforted me—or maybe it did at the time. I just know that, if he said it to me now, I'd probably tell him, "Fat lot of good that does me, Jim," since I discovered that sorry doesn't count for much up against what he put me up against.

Then, I remember snippets of this bizarre conversation with my father the next morning in which he kept telling me what I would naturally want, namely, to pick out the casket. I grant you I was on edge, but it was characteristic of a lifetime of conversations between us—during which he'd tell me what I felt whether or not it bore any relationship to what I actually felt. As I told my sister a year or two ago, when talking to him, it's best to spare oneself the aggravation of putting together coherent thoughts in an effort to communicate and simply to hum, then ask him what he heard. She shrieked with laughter, screaming, "That's it! That's it!"

Anyway, that morning I finally said through clenched teeth, "There is no way I can go pick out a *coffin* for my son," and since

I'm sure I said it in my mother's most dangerous tone of voice, he backed off. He mumbled that he'd get my brother to go with him and choose one. He did and they wound up in a fight because my father (thinking he was footing the bill) wanted one of the cheapest ones. This was finally broken up by my niece's screaming and sobbing over their having picked this time to fight battle #6,859 in *their* war.

I relate this story to illustrate that acute grief seldom brings out the best in people—and that it is absolutely guaranteed to exacerbate long-standing problems. Forget this pulling-together crap. The only people who can pull together are those who were on the same side in the first place.

The chronology of those days is jumbled. I arrived home on Friday night and Jim was buried Monday or Tuesday—I don't honestly remember which. I remember reading the obituary and discovering that my father (who was the source of the information) had left out Jim's father, grandmother, half-brother, stepsisters, aunt, uncle, and cousin as survivors. One whole side of his family eliminated from the public statement of who and what he'd been. His "people" just as much as we were.

You cannot explain thoughtlessness as deep as my father's, and you grow weary of apologizing for it when it has nothing to do with you. I called them and lied, saying that my niece, who hadn't known them, was the person who gave the paper the information. Better an oversight than an insult; better oblivious youth rather than ripened selfishness.

I do not like my father. That isn't so terrible. You wouldn't like him either if you knew him as well as I do. If you knew him less well, you'd think he was a prince of a guy. Take a poll in San Angelo, Texas, and that would be the consensus. Scotty's a prince of a guy.

The odd thing is that I recognize there's a certain truth in that. Some people are great at a public persona but stink when it comes to their private one. Other people are just the opposite.

There are fewer of them, of course, but they do exist. And God bless the child who's got both—he or she is in possession of that most elusive commodity—an integrated personality.

The difficulty of assembling all that manifested itself in Jim. It just took a different form. He was enormously likable, but people were aware that they didn't truly know him. As his chief pallbearer said when my sister asked how well he knew him: "As well as he wanted me to." He was the same with us, as dear and lovable as he was a chimera.

Dazzle in, dazzle out.

How do I account for that? Painstakingly. Give me a few hundred pages.

One thing I'll tell you right up front, though. His story and, by necessity, mine, are unique. Yet they are the story of every suicide, of every tragedy, of every dark and dangerous unattended ache the soul is heir to. Don't let anybody give you platitudes or easy answers. Don't dismiss the impulse or act of suicide as "crazy" and tell yourself you're protected because (a) you're not crazy and (b) neither are the people you love.

Get over the notion that it never makes sense, because it always makes sense to those who do it. They're just solving a problem, albeit in a way that creates a host of problems for those who are left behind. You can fault their logic all you like; you can point out that there were a plethora of other options they could have taken. But, recognize that they picked the option they did. *They* picked it, not you.

# THREE

# The First Goodbye

SOME MEMORIES ARE PERMANENTLY seared into my brain. One is standing, looking down at my son in his casket. I felt Tom, my sister Peggy, and my brother-in-law withdraw, leaving me alone with his body. I already thought of it that way. His body. Not him, not my Jimbo, Jimmy, Jim. I alarmed Peggy later, saying, "That's not him." She thought I meant I didn't think it was Jim's body, that somehow a ringer had been substituted and my son was off somewhere, alive and happy. I explained that I meant everything I knew as Jim was gone.

I stood there, noting the swollen look of his right eye and temple, realizing with horrible clarity that what I saw was likely some type of putty, molded carefully so that I, his mother, wouldn't see that part of his beloved head was missing. It even managed to irk me that they hadn't combed his hair the way he combed it, and I noticed that he'd cut it the shortest I'd seen it since he was small. I thought of the way I'd squabbled with my mother over his desire to wear his hair semi-long. She'd bait me with, "What do you think of *that hair?*"

I'd look up, see Jim get ready for the zillionth lecture on hair length and say, "Looks clean to me," before I'd go back to perusing a magazine.

Once, when her tactics wore super-thin with me, I did one of my stand-stock-still-and-look-straight-in-the-eyes thing (which signals danger to anybody who knows me) and said, "Mother, I don't care if he grows it down to his butt as long as he keeps it clean. It's *his* hair and my only concern is lice."

I should add that I remember it so well because getting the best of my mother in an argument has historically been a rare event.

I stood there, looking at Jim's body as my eyes partially filled with tears. I didn't spill a single one; there's a level of pain past which you can't do that. Tears are so precious at that level that you can't let go of them. They're all you have. As I watched him, my heartbeat caused the tears to pulsate rhythmically and my mind split in two. One half saw my son moving and said, "It's all been a mistake." The other half knew exactly what I was doing and said, "Just because you'd like to believe that doesn't make it so."

I put my hand on his chest. I didn't want to touch his flesh, couldn't deal with the coldness and firmness I knew I'd find. His chest was enough. I was touching him, but I couldn't feel him. I couldn't bear to feel him.

The Biblical phrase came back to me—"flesh of my flesh." That was why I couldn't feel him. It would have been my dead flesh and it would have been the flesh which came from mine; flesh which my fingertips vividly remembered caressing. Better the remembered tingle of soft baby skin than the reality of his corpse. My corpse.

And, while I find it ironic that I would think of another Biblical phrase, I also heard the echo of David's cry—"O my son Absalom, my son, my son Absalom! Would God I had died for thee, O Absalom, my son, my son!"

Yes. Would God I had died for thee.

Then, in one of those flashes of insight so profound that it took years for the rest of my brain and heart to catch up with it, I told him very softly, so softly that only he could hear—and then only if he bent close—"I gave you life. But, once I did, it belonged to you." I was saying that it had been his choice, but it would have never been mine. I think I knew that, from that moment on, all I could do was work on forgiving him for it.

I patted his chest, then touched his hair and left.

I realized later that, at the funeral, I was expected to seat myself at the end of the pew, the rest of the family filing past me. I didn't. I walked to the far end of the pew so that no one could come near me but Tom, and I sat so that he was between me and everybody else. That was exactly how I wanted it. I wanted neither to give nor to receive comfort at that point. I just wanted a corner and a shield—and I made damn sure I got them. Isn't it amazing how our instincts work when our brain doesn't?

I also deliberately didn't wear my glasses. I wanted to see the faces of those who came close to me, but I wanted everything else to have the soft blur of an astigmatic world.

It was such a cold, gray day—at a time of year which is often balmy and bright in Texas. And I said (in the car, following the hearse) that it was such an ugly day and I was glad, since I couldn't have stood for it to be pretty.

But, of course, standing what I did, I could have stood that.

When we were at the graveside, I sat between Tom and Jim's father, Garland. I think Tom took my hand and that I took Garland's. My awareness then (and my memory now) has a split-screen telephoto and closeup shot of that—me sitting there between my first and third husbands, holding hands with both of them and feeling the strength flow from Tom to me, from me to Garland. It felt very natural and it felt like a perfect metaphor for my relationship with each of them. Tom always gave to me; I always gave to Garland.

I remember looking at the pallbearers and trying to reassure them with my expression. I'm not sure what I was reassuring them of—maybe that I wasn't going to get hysterical and burden them with my grief, heaping it on top of theirs. Maybe it was an effort to tell them that his death wasn't their fault. I did know that. Especially since, at that point, I felt it was entirely mine.

I worried about the bitter cold. The moment the service was over and the pallbearers walked back to the hearse, I got up and started for them. Tom could barely keep up with me as I murmured, "The sooner I go, the sooner everybody gets out of the cold. But, I want to thank them." I did, shaking their hands and saying simply to each of them, "Thank you for doing this for Jim." I only knew two of them and wouldn't recognize any of the rest if I saw them today. They were just young faces—troubled, pained, embarrassed young faces. I think every maternal instinct in me was responding to them, needing to take care of them in lieu of the son I would never take care of again.

Before I could leave the cemetery, however, a woman came up to me and said her name, that she worked in a restaurant I recognized as the one where Jim used to eat breakfast most mornings. (He told me when he confessed he didn't ever use the coffeemaker I gave him.) She said, "My son killed himself when he was nineteen. I know how you feel."

I thanked her and I hugged her and I tried to feel comforted by a kindred spirit, but my brain was saying, "No, you don't. Nobody knows how I feel but me." Grief is so common. And at 50,000 people a year in America alone, suicide is so common. She believed that she knew what I felt, but she was simply remembering her own feelings during *her* son's funeral.

But my son was unique, just as I am unique, just as our relationship was unique. And her son was unique, she is unique, and their relationship was unique. Still, I thank that dear lady, whoever and wherever she is. Hers was an act of kindness and compassion. If there's somebody listening who bestows blessings, I hope She/He sends her one.

Right after the funeral, Tom said something which meant nothing at the time and a whale of a lot in the years to come. He said, "He would have been so proud of you. You gave his death dignity."

I'm still hard pressed to explain why that's important, but I suspect it has to do with the tradition of shamefulness, the culturally implanted notion that suicide is a "sin" and, therefore, morally reprehensible. I figure about thirty-nine people in the world know that neither the Old nor the New Testament directly forbids suicide. The Christian prohibition on it dates from the fourth century and was enunciated by St. Augustine, who was simply concerned about the ever-thinning ranks of Christians who either were seeking martyrdom or were religious zealots bent on getting to Heaven without passing Go. He didn't say a word about those who committed suicide because of physical or emotional suffering, old age, altruism toward others, personal honor, illness, and the like—the reasons which explain 99.9 percent of suicides today.

I have several theories on how Augustine's moral interpretation became "gospel." Part of it is that, in any illiterate society, the word of an authority is given the same credibility as the written word and soon becomes confused with it. The fact that it's never been straightened out hinges on several aspects of both human nature and American society. One is that we are functionally illiterate, meaning nobody in America reads much of anything, let alone the Bible. Most of us have read parts of it; few of us have read all of it. And unless you have (and have a very good memory), you don't know what's *not* there any more than you know what is.

The second factor is that people have always thought that, if a little of anything is good, a whole lot of it is better. The tendency is always to overstate whatever we believe—I suppose it's a way of locking it in—and if suicide is prohibited in some circumstances, that soon becomes generalized to all circumstances.

Finally, if you look at history, it becomes abundantly clear that people have always thought that everybody else should believe the way they do and will ram it down the others' throat, given the opportunity.

There you have my theory of why a highly specific edict, issued by a fourth-century cleric to a very narrow audience, has become the commonly accepted and (erroneously) "Bible-sanctioned" principle that "anybody who commits suicide goes straight to Hell." To say that I don't buy it is to carry understatement to the level of the ludicrous.

Not that I haven't been grateful for my patients' ignorance of the facts. Time and again I've been told that the unthinkable consequence (roasting in Hell) was the only thing that stopped my patient from following through with a plan to kill him or herself. Believe me, I do not disabuse them of the notion. What ever keeps us in the fray. . . .

Anyway, since I had no sense of Jim's act as a "sin," I wasn't ashamed on that score. And at the time of his funeral, shame over my contribution to his death paled in comparison to the devastation I felt. *That* was my most immediate concern—how to live with that. I couldn't think of anything I'd ever be able to plug up that hole with—anything that would ever give me back a semblance of control.

I had gotten through the loss of my beloved brother-in-law five years earlier by writing some prose about him that was read at his funeral. Tom encouraged me to do a similar thing for Jim's funeral and kept telling me I *could,* even though I kept saying I *couldn't.*

As usual, he was right.

This time, my grief came out in the form of a poem. I wasn't able to read it aloud though, and a minister who knew Jim did. I assure you no award-winning actor or poet could have done a better job. I still thank him from the bottom of my heart for the full, rich feeling with which he read:

Why did you go, Jim?
Like liquid sunshine you slipped through my fingers
And left me with my guilt and anger and love
Why *this* choice and not a million others?

It is so like you somehow
To leave no margin for error
A hunter who finally stalked himself
And, sighting his wounded quarry,
Decided to end its suffering

You were always, always a person
And told me so at the age of three
Yes, you were, and as long as I live you shall be
For I liked the person you were
Almost as much as I loved you

You are gone
And you are with me
I carried and I carry you inside me
Even though you aborted my future
          with your precious, beloved self

I will always feel I failed you
But I am grateful anyway
For I know that love can outlast pain
And I will turn to others to endure what
          I cannot endure alone
I love you, Jim, my son
I love you

Like any poem, some things are expressed directly while others require reading between the lines. I'll try to tell you what lay between the lines in this book, but it'll take me awhile.

I had Peggy, my brother David, and Tom to help me through the worst of the grief. To a lesser extent, I had my niece and some friends. I did not have my parents. I was very confused about whether or not I wanted them anyway, so that was okay with me.

I'm pretty sure they were racked by guilt. I can't say I worried a lot about that at the time, having all I could do to deal with my own.

I did try to console my father the first or second morning. I leaned over and put my arms around him. He didn't respond, waiting until I sat down to tell me that he'd known Jim was going to do it, that Jim had been telling him for a year he felt like it. My father got teary-eyed, saying, "When the police car pulled up, I knew he'd finally done it. I realized I'd been waiting for them all that time." He added that I mustn't despair, because he knew Jim was now in Heaven with the angels, since he was "saved." Then he quoted King David, who, after his young son died (not the more relevant Absalom, I thought bitterly), refused to mourn, saying that it was pointless since his son would not return to him but he would someday go to him. My father said, "I'll go to him," and I thought how thrilled Jim was going to be to see him, but said, "Excuse me," getting up and going into Jim's bedroom where, shaking violently, I called my sister and said, "I need you to get over here *right now.*" I felt like killing my father and Peggy seemed like the only person who could stop me.

That sounds dreadful, doesn't it? It's what I felt like though— what I still feel like, remembering his words as they struck me like hammer blows. Hearing that he'd had a year's warning but never saw fit to call me and tell me my son was that despondent. Hearing the old, old message that the important thing was pie-in-the-sky-by-and-by and not taking constructive action to resolve the emotional crisis at hand. Hearing that he was, in essence, denying his heavy contribution to Jim's suicide. Hearing the complete, utter discounting of both my feelings and experience that lay behind his words.

Let me explain that.

I had always shown what I considered the proper respect for my father's religious beliefs, but he'd known for years that I didn't share them. My own beliefs aren't a function of ignorance but of having synthesized a philosophy and spirituality which make abundant sense to me and which cause all dogma to send me off the deep end. I have a number of minister friends and I frequently surprise them with my Biblical knowledge. They say I'm a very good theologian.

I've also done the fundamentalist course—attended church three times a week, taught Sunday School, got "saved," back-slid and "rededicated" myself (thankfully, I got all this out of my system early). Now, nothing exasperates me more than people who not only are totally enchanted with their own religious system but also think they're on a mission from God with a specific injunction to *make* everybody else agree with them. I feel like a friend's father who joked, "I haven't been a Democrat since I learned to read." You might say that I haven't been into formal religion (as opposed to spirituality) since I learned to read outside my own "born-again Christian" religion.

I didn't proselytize my ideology to my father, but he asked me questions sometimes—did I believe in Heaven, Satan, etc.? I answered him honestly, but added that I thought people ought to hold onto whatever helps them. I neither expected nor asked him to see spiritual matters my way. His words that morning reminded me that he'd never return the courtesy.

Also, when I say he denied my experience, I refer to the fact that I am not only a psychiatrist, but a Menninger-trained psychiatrist—meaning that I did my training at one of the best psychiatric institutions in the world. I was undeniably Jim's mother and not his psychiatrist—I wouldn't even have tried to take that role. But I would have known the "system" and could have gotten him the kind of help he needed. My father's omission (which was based on contempt for my profession since he's certain you just need to "get right with God" and everything will be hunky-dory) guaranteed that I never had the chance.

You are, of course, wondering why Jim didn't tell me how he was feeling himself. I think the answer is best summed up by something Peggy said. I asked her the question you're asking now, and she responded, "Jim had the relationship with you he wanted."

Yes. I had been Jim's weird Mom, fulfilling all the Mom functions (and most of the Dad ones too) as he grew up, but also being a freshman college student and his Cub Scout den mother the same year, heading off to medical school as he started high school, always being mistaken for his older sister, cracking up at his witticisms, sharing major decisions with him. We have this odd notion we only give to our children. We're oblivious to how much they give to us. Once I was so discouraged I couldn't summon a shred of belief in myself. I asked aloud what I thought I was doing, trying to get into medical school when I was just this stupid klutz who'd messed up every important thing in her life. Jim, nearly thirteen, plunked down beside me, put his arm around me, and said, "Mom, you're just tired and you're trying to do too much. Take a breather. Drop those night courses you're taking and do them when you're not working so many hours." When I didn't say anything, he added, "You're going to be a terrific doctor. One thing, though. I think you should reconsider and go into surgery instead of family medicine."

I looked at him, curious, and asked, "Why?"

He grinned and answered, "Oh, you know. Cutting and sewing is woman's work."

I started gurgling with laughter. He added, "And think about it. You could put up some of your needlework in your waiting room—let people pick their favorite stitch—it'd give you a real edge on the competition."

Is that a treasured memory? Yes. It is also an important memory, because I characteristically do a lousy job of either soliciting or accepting reassurance. I needed the infusion of Jim's love and humor and belief in me—and, knowing me, he knew the format most likely to succeed. I tried always to pay him back in kind. That was the relationship with me he wanted, the one Peggy referred to. Still, I think Jim sensed that, in my own deepest despair, I had not and would not burden him with it—that even though I had shared the crisis I described above with him, there were other, more profound crises in my life which I handled as best I could, leaving him out of it. I think that, in feeling suicidal for a year but choosing not to tell me, he was trying to do the same.

I knew he was depressed. It came across in his voice, in the words he chose. But he'd describe his frustration with my father's back-stabbing and constant carping, his backaches (See what I mean about psychosomatic illness? My Dad was always on his back, was breaking his back, was stabbing him in the back), his money troubles—and, if I started to sound alarmed, he'd begin to joke, painting hysterical vignettes of life in the Scott household. (For example, my mother's an infamous nag, and he told her once to put it all on tape so he could portion it out in accordance with how much he could stand at the moment.)

I worried incessantly about his inability to get out on his own. I understood the financial basis for it, knew that Jim's training and job experience lay in welding and things related to the oil industry—which was in a major, major slump in the 1980s. He was good at sales, but he couldn't get past the low wages of an entry job. Most people with a high-paying skill are caught in that trap. If the economy won't support the full-time exercise of their skill, they have a hard time not feeling that they've lost their value too. A low-paying job seems to verify that they're not worth as much. That's pretty hard to take.

I also knew that, as an only child, Jim was a natural isolate and that my parents were the most stable form of family he'd known. They kept him connected with cousins, aunts, uncles—part of a matrix that gave him a sense of who he was and where he belonged in the world. I had married his father at fifteen (Garland was eighteen), divorced him when I was nineteen, and remarried the same year. Jim's stepfather adopted him since he was only two when we married, but I divorced that "Dad" after nine years, and he and Jim gradually drifted away from each other.

I think both that drift and Jim's identification with my parents was what led him to have his name changed to Scott when he was fifteen. It was four years following the divorce and he asked me if I was as tired of having people slaughter our last name (which was German and difficult) as he was. When I said yes, he suggested we petition for a name change and become Scotts at the same time. He argued that there were frequent hassles associated with the fact that he was living with his grandparents but had a different last name. The same name would simplify both his life and theirs. I remember teasing him, saying, "Having your mother's maiden name is bound to suggest your birth came about under less than ideal circumstances."

He laughed, answering that Garland was more likely to be embarrassed about it than he was, especially since a casual glance at the two of them was enough to establish paternity.

That whole thing was, I think, very telling about Jim's wry sense of humor—a sense of humor very like my own and one which had a strong iconoclastic streak and dictated that pomposity (whether in oneself or others) *ought* to be punctured. That goes down to the bone and asserts that appearances mean very damn little. I've looked great and known I was totally screwed; I've looked like an erratic dingbat and known I was solid as a rock. Jim always responded to me as the latter. I tried to hide the former, and being a considerate son, he pretended I'd gotten by with it.

Sometimes that's what people who love each other do. They know each other's flaws and what needs work, but they also know unconditional love is vital to us sometimes; we need it infinitely more than constructive criticism. I believed Jim needed my encouragement and blind faith in him, so I kept my silence about all the problems he never seemed to solve. Sometimes he had done the same for me. I think that was our "deal" and that both of us had the relationship we wanted.

I would say my silence had terrible consequences in this instance, but the truth is that no suicide is so simple. Even if it was a
factor, I don't know how much weight it carried. I also don't
know how much sense it makes to beat up on myself for doing
something I categorically believe in.

Sometimes Jim left me alone. Sometimes I left him alone. It's
called giving each other space. And so, I believe, it should be. I
may question whether I gave him too much space or why I placed
such a premium on it (actually, I know that one—it was crucial to
me because my mother never seemed to get out of my face).

But that consequent distance led me to write in the journal I
kept after Jim's death, "By the time I knew he was dying, he was
dead."

# FOUR

# Journaling
# to Survive

THERE ARE A NUMBER OF ENTRIES in that journal I want to share
with you now. They start on November 26, 1984, ten days after
Jim died, and I'll simply put them in the sequence they're recorded.

**11–26–84**   Among his things I found his high school
diploma and invitation. Jumbled in with those were the
invitation to my medical school graduation and the an-
nouncement of my residency graduation. In the midst of
these few "treasures" was a program for a college awards
night—and, each time my name was mentioned, he had
marked it. He had saved it since 1971.

I sat there holding it and crying. Crying because my
son was proud of me, prouder of me than himself. I would
give anything if it had been the other way around.

**11–27–84**   One Christmas, 700 miles apart, we bought
each other identical chains. I opened his and had a moment of confusion, thinking I'd somehow mailed his gift
back to myself. We laughed about it and I said something

about his exquisite taste and "great minds running in the same channels."

I found the chain in his room. With it was a "dogtag" with his name on it, another present from me. Aside from cufflinks and a tie pin, it was the only jewelry in his room. He'd really worn this chain. It's tarnished with body oil—not dirty, but with his chemistry embedded.

My thought when I found it and brought it home was that I would clean it up and wear it, but I know now that it's far more precious to me as is.

I can't decide about wearing mine.

There's something so moving about seeing them side by side. I had some links cut out of mine when I first got it so that it would be a choker, so his is much bigger.

He was always so solid, my son. The family called him my "sponge rubber baby" with his chunky little legs and dimples for knuckles.

He never got any taller than me and his hair was never quite as dark and our smiles were the same and his eyes were a blend of his father's and mine.

And I love him and I miss him and I would give up anything, including my own life, if it would only bring him back.

**11–29–84**    I lay down (I am so everlastingly *tired*) and had the strangest feeling I was Jim. My face on the pillow was his face and if my eyes opened they would have been his eyes. I felt my shoulders broader, my weight against the bed greater, my hair lighter and curlier.

Isn't it supposed to be the other way around? Our parents inside of us? I don't know that I ever thought about it except in a more abstract way.

Maybe that's what grief does—makes reality of abstractions.

This is a very bad day.

Last Thursday was Thanksgiving, so I was preoccupied with that. Today the thought is unavoidable—"two weeks ago today, Jim was living out his last 24 hours."

I torment myself with the thoughts that were running through his mind and, like someone probing an open wound, I picture that last split-second. Was he crying? Did he say anything, like, "I'm sorry, Mom?" Were his eyes open or closed? I don't know why those things matter and I know that they'll never be answered. I only hope that someday I'll stop wondering.

I dreamed about him last night and I wish I believed in dreams in the prophetic sense. Because he was there, he came back from the dead to tell me he was all right and that I must not worry about him. He said he'd married a girl named Marian and they were expecting a baby. I don't remember saying a thing, only his words and the feel of his hand on my shoulder.

Oh, Jim—sometimes those are the only two words my lacerated soul can manage. Oh, Jim . . .

"To be gifted but not to know how best to make use of one's gifts, to be highly ambitious but at the same time to feel unworthy, is a dangerous combination which can often end in mental breakdown or suicide."*

"The psychoanalytic treatment method is a great discovery but this is not what changed psychiatry. It was the new understanding that psychoanalytic research gave us concerning men's motives and inner resources, the intensity of partially buried conflicts, the unknown and unplumbed depths and heights of our nature, the formidable power each of us holds to determine whether he

*W. H. Auden, foreword, in *Markings,* by Dag Hammarskjold (New York: Knopf, 1980).

lives or dies. It was the realization that we must encourage each individual to see himself not as a mere spectator of cosmic events but as a prime mover; to regard himself not as a passive incident in the infinite universe but as one important unit possessing the power to influence great decisions by making small ones."*

12–1–84    It's December now, Jim. A December you'll never see. A December without you in it for me. I wasn't going to see you this Christmas—it's my turn to take call—and I remember wondering if that was a factor, but decided I was being grandiose.

The last two lines of your note read, "My dreams and ambitions require more than I can give. The damn problem is that I have found people believe in themselves and what they are doing in life"

There is no period at the (seeming) end of that sentence, son, but I think I know how it ends: ". . . and I don't—I don't believe in myself or what I'm doing with my life."

I feel responsible for that—and, yet, I know how many times and how many ways I tried to help you do just that.

You suffered mainly by comparison to *me* and the guilt of that has nearly torn me apart for years. I said to Peggy, "Maybe if I hadn't needed to achieve so much, maybe if I'd stayed home and never even gone to college, never been a doctor?" And she answered with love and honesty, "He was proud of you, Sis. And even if you had stayed home and done none of the things you've done, it wouldn't have changed anything. Everybody, including Jim, would know how smart you are."

---

*Karl Menninger, "Hope," address before the 115th Annual Meeting of the American Psychiatric Association, 1959.

But there's smart and there's smart—and it drove me crazy that you could never see that, never believe that you were superior to me in other ways. All my efforts to tell you felt brushed aside and you heard as patronizing what I meant as a loan of confidence. I was trying to say, "I believe in you, Jim. I'm proud of you. Please believe in yourself as I do."

I keep having this crazy thought about my pregnancy with you—and I don't know if it puts me more on the hook or takes me off and puts your father on.

It goes like this—I was desperately unhappy. I think I cried everyday. I kept going over and over the things he had said to me: that he would never love you, that the sight of me disgusted him, that you were *my* baby, not his, because I wanted you, not him. And I would go in what became your room and take out your soft baby clothes and cry and make promises to you. Promises that I would love you enough for both of us, that even though I wasn't much, I was going to try as hard as I could to be a good mother to you.

The thought I have now is that I damaged you in some fundamental way. That my anguish was laid down with your bones and lay dormant all these years, only to erupt in that single, devastating act of self-destruction.

I feel I poisoned you, son. That I gave you my self-doubt and pain, transmitted directly from me to you, but without the genes to hold on. Without my stubbornness and tenacity. Should I have made you a Taurus like me instead of a tender-hearted little crab? But you see—I didn't plan your birth—and even if I had, I'd have tried to improve on myself and picked a different month.

Now I can't imagine you different than you were. Your flaws were fatal to you, but to me they were unimportant compared to the rest of you.

My anger at you is still dampened. Mainly it has to do with feeling cheated. You robbed me of your company, of that special connection between mother and son, of your easy laugh and the slight awkwardness of our hugs. You've cheated some young woman of loving and being loved by you. You've cheated me of learning what sort of mother-in-law I'd be, of testing certain limits in myself. And second only to the pain of losing you, you've saddled me with the pain of losing my grandchildren, because now they'll never exist.

Ironic, isn't it? My hobby in genealogy and I always conceptualized our family as an unbroken chain. A direct line, passing down through time, through me, through you. You've broken that chain, Jim. My last link snapped off with you.

Well, maybe it's time. I don't feel too worthy of perpetuation right now, anyway.

I was thinking about the term "psychological autopsy"—a wonderful euphemism invented by some shrink to describe the process of sifting through "post mortem psychological evidence" (often of suicides) looking for an explanation or theory that fits the known facts.

In a sense, it's what I'm doing, but I find the term macabre. I only wondered about it for a moment—why we invented such a term—then it hit me. Self-protection. We do it to distance ourselves from death and, maybe more to the point, to distance ourselves from the "death wish," man's self-destructiveness.

I'm certainly not discovering anything new—it's just that my odyssey is so personal. Jim's not a case study to me—he was a baby in my arms, an infectious laugh, a thousand freeze-frame pictures in my mind, so many tender moments, so many flashes of mutual feeling, a kindred spirit, my biggest encourager at times I needed encouragement, a consideration in all my major decisions, part of my everyday thoughts from the time he was conceived.

He fits a kind of classic picture, even down to inheriting my tendency toward depression. But he wasn't a classic case—he was my son and I feel responsible while, at the same time, I can't see how I could have followed through with all the desperate measures that now occur to me.

**12–2–84** In a letter to a friend whose son had died, Sigmund Freud said, "We find a place for what we lose. Although we know that after such a loss the acute stage of mourning will subside, we also know that we shall remain inconsolable and will never find a substitute. No matter what may fill the gap, even if it be filled completely, it nevertheless remains something else."*

I'm so glad you existed—even if it was too short a time for me and too long a time for you.

I'm glad I had you. I'm glad my memories are full of you. I'm glad you gave me a chance to know what it means to be a mother. I think you were great for *my* development, even if I wasn't so great for yours.

I'm sorry I was such a jerk sometimes. I'm sorry I wasn't more patient. I'm sorry I spanked and yelled at you. I'm sorry for every critical remark or attitude.

Mea culpa, mea culpa, mea maxima culpa.

I wish there were Somebody around who could forgive me—Nobody could be harsher than me.

**12–4–84** Today is my favorite niece, Vona's, birthday. Maybe you're not "supposed to" have favorites, but I do. Fate (or whatever) decreed that my sister and I would

*E. L. Freud, ed., *Letters of Sigmund Freud* (New York: Basic Books, 1961).

only have one child apiece—she had the girl, I had the boy, and each of us got a taste of being pseudo-Mom to a little person the opposite sex to our own child.

She's very dear to me. And, I admire her—far more than Peggy or me, she does what she wants to and doesn't do what she doesn't want to. I guess that's "assertiveness" in the best sense—because she is loving and responsible with it.

She gave according to my need.

In the past, each time I went home, Peggy and I got a bag of our favorite candy and we'd eat it together—one of those family rituals that makes your heart smile because it has meanings you don't need to say.

And this time, Vona walked in and handed me a bag of that candy. I thanked her and I hugged her, but I thought she was crazy. Every bite that went in my mouth took an effort—and she brought me *candy!?*

The thought got lost in the shuffle, but she sat by my chair for hours, touching me. Every now and then I'd lean toward her, tease her with a pet name, hug her and get hugged back.

She drove the car from the funeral home to the cemetery. I wasn't sure why—maybe there was a practical reason—but seeing her at the wheel, her eyes red but dry—kept my own strength available to me. And it felt so right.

I don't know when I finally understood the candy. And maybe I don't understand yet all the levels of meaning—just as I don't understand all the levels of bonding that makes up a family.

I do understand that I love her very much.

**12–6–84**    I dreamed about Jim again last night. I was at my parents' house, getting ready to leave (and return to what has become "home" now that the place I always called home has become "my parents' house"). I don't remember any words, just a feeling of joy at my departure. I went into some unknown room and found a huge stainless steel chest (like his stainless steel coffin) with racks in it (nine of them—like a three dimensional tic-tac-toe grid). There was a man in the second rack on the lefthand side and I knew it was my father from the bald spot on top of his head. And in the top slot on the righthand side was my Jim, his head misshapen by the gunshot, but not bloody (the reverse of "my head is bloody, but not bowed?") and still unmistakably him. He turned over within that small space and look directly at me. He said, "I'm all right, Mom. Really. I'm all right." And, I started to say, "Jim, I'm sorry I left you with them." He looked angry or impatient and said, "I've got to go now," then he and the other man disappeared.

And that's the way it is—I'm left with all my apologies and guilt to contend with. I feel like he left angrily, impatiently—unwilling to listen, unwilling to work out some compromise.

I saw a man once whose brother had committed suicide. All he needed to know was that his feelings were normal. He said something that stuck in my mind, something that captured the essence of the frustration suicide survivors feel. He said, "He ended the dialogue. Now I only have my half of the argument."

**12–8–84** My mother called me last night. I answered that I was all right, that I had my good days and bad days. I asked after her and my Dad. She said, "I thought at first he wasn't going to make it. He's grieving him so." She paused and began to cry, then went on, "I see him everywhere I turn." There was another pause, then, "I'm not helping *you*. I'd better go."

I said, "It's all right, Mom. I appreciate your concern.
Thank you for calling me."

"Well, I'd better go."

I felt pity, but it was really all I felt. The kind of pity
you have for strangers.

I don't have the kind of anger that makes you lash
out. I don't even have the kind that makes you falsely
benevolent. I have the kind that severs whatever was
there before. I think that's the reason my father was in
the steel box with Jim in my dream. I think he's now dead
for me.

It's a relief in a way.

I know that my parents love me—at least they love
the me they think I am. But I don't like them and I don't
think they like me.

I guess only time will reveal whether or not my parents are still my parents, whether or not we're still connected, whether or not our "relatedness" is more than a
mere decision.

I found my life insurance policy in his things. It still
had my note in it. It says, "Jim, This policy is made out to
you and I thought it should probably be in your possession
in case I croak while traveling or something. I love you,
Mom."

It looked like it had fallen in a mud puddle. But, then,
Jim's room *was* a mud puddle.

It was the strangest thing. He was absolutely fastidi-
ous about his person. His hair was always clean, he
seemed to change clothes several times a day, he often
bathed morning and night. But his room was a disaster.

Peggy was appalled by the state of his room—thinking it reflected the level of his depression. If so, then he
was depressed a long, long time. I nagged and ranted and

raved, threatened to throw out his things time and time again. I gave up straightening drawers when he was nine. It was just in the nick of time, because he told me later that he'd kept a dead snake in one for a while after that.

When he was ten, I gave up entirely on his room. I pulled the vacuum cleaner up to his door and I said, "From now on, kid, you're on your own." I told him that I'd wash his things, but I wasn't going in his room any more unless it was to take laundry in or out. I decided to enjoy him outside that room, to let it be his business. I didn't want to be a shrieking harridan, like I felt my mother had been.

I don't know if it was the right thing. Now I wonder if I should have seen it as a symptom—seen it as a sign of Jim's divided nature and helped him more with the forces of chaos.

God, I wish I'd been wiser.

# FIVE

# Reorienting

WE DO WHAT WE CAN to reorient ourselves. And make no mistake about it, when you lose your loved one to suicide, you *need* reorienting. A two-by-four upside the head is a mild shock comparatively speaking.

I returned to Clear Lake the Wednesday before Thanksgiving, and since the office was closed Thursday and Friday, I decided it was a good time for me to go in. I wanted to be alone in that setting, to do what I could to start the reorienting process. Once I was there, I sat at my desk for a while, looking at the papers and messages on it. One of my co-workers had left a small brochure about the aftermath of suicide. I read it with great interest and was a little comforted by it, since it made unusual reactions normal and sort of "de-crazied" me. Then I got up and slowly walked into each person's office. I didn't touch anything, didn't say anything. I just stood in each room, coming back to the person who occupied it. I pictured each of them—not reacting to my tragedy, just going about their work, speaking to me about cases, asking and answering. I don't know why doing that was important to me. I guess I was just trying to make things ordinary again. Now I was in *this* world, *this* time. Not the world of pain and loss which kept crushing the breath out of me when I tried to comb my hair or feed my cat. This was my work world. The place where I knew what to do.

Somehow my boss, Ken, knew I'd need that kind of reorienting too—a chance to wade a little, since the stunned muscles wouldn't remember how to swim—and he arranged for all of us to meet the following Sunday at his house, in a way to "sit shiva," that ritual of remembrance of the deceased and low expectations of the bereaved which makes Judaism sometimes feel so much more human than Christianity. He gave me the clear message that we would do whatever I wanted and I elected to take some poems and one prose piece, then to have each of my friends read one. Three of them were Whitman's: "There Was a Child Went Forth," "Who Learns My Lessons Complete?" and "Assurances." I recommend them to you. The prose was taken from Mark Twain's "Letters from the Earth," and it is a hysterically funny lampooning of (among other things) the concept of Heaven. I also recommend it to you. If it shocks you, you're overdue to read it. But be of good cheer. In the words of Freud, "The best achievements in the way of jokes are used as an envelope for thoughts of the greatest substance."* (He was a big fan of Twain's, by the way.) It nails down in a compelling way all those things you've always known were irrational but were encouraged/required to swallow whole when you were a kid. It puts your feet on firmer ground, having Mark Twain validate your experience and tell you it's okay to use your brain when thinking about spiritual matters.

I say I provided those things for my friends to read as though I planned all that. I didn't. I took those things along thinking that might be what I wanted but knowing that what I wanted changed from moment to moment and that, if anything characterized my thoughts, it was their scattered quality. If you pictured someone drifting through a room, picking up first this object, then another, carrying them a few paces, turning, putting them back, hesitating, moving forward, retracing steps, then you'd have a mental image of the way my mind worked—which is to say, not too efficiently.

I am used to being mentally sharp, having flashes of insight,

*Sigmund Freud, *Jokes and Their Relation to the Unconscious* (New York: Norton, 1960).

sometimes dazzling people with the quickness with which I grasp subtleties. It's disruptive to lose that edge; it makes you question who you are and whether or not you'll ever be the same. It's another punch at a time you're still reeling from a technical knockout. And I have little patience with myself in general. As you might imagine, I wasn't patient with myself for functioning as though my brain were bogged down in molasses.

I was also very, very scared. Before going back to work, I wrote in my journal: "I keep telling myself that I'll have to watch every impulse, weigh every word. In a sense, I always do, but when I'm functioning normally, it's often an instantaneous process—I know I can't rely on that being there now. God, I don't want to damage my patients—contaminate them with my defensiveness and grief."

The defensiveness was about my concern that my colleagues might judge me deficient—how could a credible psychiatrist have a son who killed himself?—but I had enough rationality left to know that they were more likely to evaluate my competence on the basis of *their* interactions with me rather than of a complicated event they knew little about. I both expected and got greater understanding and tolerance than I think the "average" survivor does. Then again, I was more prone to ask for it. There were two people in the clinic I especially leaned on. I didn't do it often, but when I hit my limit, I knew I could go to either of them and say whatever I had to say without worrying about how it sounded. I don't remember the words they said back; I just know they communicated their belief that I was doing a remarkable job of surviving. Their every interaction with me said, "Way to go, Sue!"

I decided to notify a select group of my long-distance friends by letter. I can't tell you my criteria; I just know that the list made itself and that everyone on it was someone who was important to me, whether because of shared feelings, experiences, or philosophies. The letter to them read:

At 2 A.M., Friday, November the 16th, my son, Jim, took his own life. He was in physical and mental pain for more than a year and I try to console myself with the thought that his torment is ended.

I am writing this letter to those friends I want or need to have this knowledge. Please do not call me to express your sympathy or concern—I know it's there, but my self-control is both very fragile and very important to me. If you wish to offer a memorial tribute, please make a contribution to Compassionate Friends, the organization for bereaved parents.

I am enclosing a poem which I wrote to express my grief and which was read at his funeral. Please keep it for me as a remembrance of him.

I would welcome your letters, and I will answer them when and however I can. Please do not feel you have to be profound or cautious— just be my friend as you have been in the past.

The responses were warm and loving—and, to my surprise, word spread among others who'd known me and I heard from them as well. Sometimes people said things that initially seemed stupid or self-centered—like one woman who went on and on about her frustrated efforts to adopt a child. I was able to find the gold in the grit, however, and to write back, thanking her for the reminder that I had been blessed with a child in the first place and that my loss could never completely cancel out the good that had done me. I didn't manufacture that interpretation—I know it's what she meant, what her heart was trying to say to mine.

Such messages are often like that. I would encourage any survivor to make the effort to hear what underlies poorly stated condolences. We need to realize that not everyone is emphatically gifted, that the ability not only to feel what another does but then use words which soothe and heal lies on a scale from dolt to genius. You don't judge people for where they fall on a scale. You simply note the number they're at and give them credit for trying when that number is low.

Around that time, I discovered the magic words, "No, I can't do that right now." Sounds simple, doesn't it? It's not if you've always knocked yourself out, always taken on the burdens of the world, always believed you had to hold everything together. I don't just function; typically I overfunction. I still do a lot of the time. But I also remember the magic words and say them now when things stack up and there isn't enough Sue Chance to go around.

"No, I can't do that right now."

Doesn't mean you never can. Doesn't mean you consider the request stupid or unreasonable. Doesn't mean you don't ever want to be asked again. Doesn't mean you don't value the person asking. You just can't do it right then. And I guarantee you, the more capable you are, the more you're going to need to say it sometimes. You'll be expected to do everything because, like Domino's, you're known to deliver.

It's important for you to understand, though, that if, by your nature, you're a Hero—one who habitually acts as though the bullets bounce off—you will go on doing it for the most part. The price you will pay for that is illustrated in my journal entry from November 27, 1984:

> I barely made it through the door. I guess, in fact, I didn't, since I started crying in the car. I came in, patted the cat, came upstairs and started to change, when, with one leg of my sweatsuit pants on, I began sobbing and fell over on the bed, curled up in a fetal position.
>
> All I could think was, "If you want to *really* be a failure in life, have your child commit suicide." It's bad enough to lose a child and my heart really does go out to other bereaved parents, but the guilt you have over not getting them to a doctor "soon enough," the guilt over not being able to protect them from cancer or drunk drivers or whatever can't be as fundamental and soul-searing as knowing they couldn't endure the life you gave them.

Some friends of mine distilled a concept of one of the major life-tasks of the elderly into the question, "Does my love create or destroy?" The inescapable conclusion is that mine destroys. All other "proofs" of the good that I do are overshadowed by Jim's death. It seems, in this moment of terrible despair, to cancel out all other considerations and pronounces me guilty of a wasted life.

There are moments like that when everything crashes in on you, when there's too much world at once. At such moments your own candle nearly gutters out and you consider the option your loved one took. You shriek aloud or in your mind, "I can't bear this! I can't bear this!" It feels so profoundly true.

So why, you are wondering, did I *not* opt out? Because I knew I *could* bear it, having borne other excruciating things. Because I had been abandoned and rejected before and knew (intellectually, at least) that those treacheries have almost everything to do with the traitor and virtually nothing to do with the victim. Traitors can be understood, even empathized with, but they remain traitors. As they should.

We tend to idealize the suicide, especially when he's our child. We focus on his suffering, we respond to the accusation inherent in suicide, the message that *we* failed, that we, in effect, murdered *him.* I think that comes through loud and clear in the passage I quoted above. But the reality, my friends, is that he murders *us.* We are the victims—and when you are victimized by someone pledged to the same values/system/family, you have been betrayed.

Jim was a traitor to me. He was a traitor to everyone who loved him. His act was a rejection of both the world we had chosen and the one which had chosen us. One of the Greek terms for suicide is *haireo thanaton,* and it means "to seize death." Whatever else suicide represents—and there are rational ways to understand it—the basic premise it violates is that life is preferable to death. We not only need to believe that but we have an obligation to validate it for each other. We do that by staying in the fight.

I am so exasperated by those who use the term "successful" in talking about suicide. It goes beyond mere thoughtlessness into the realm of pure stupidity. A month after Jim died, I heard an emergency room doctor refer to a spate of critical gunshot wounds and overdoses as "unsuccessful" suicides. He had no idea I had lost my son to suicide as he implied that, if people are going to do it, they ought to do it "right." I tried briefly to suggest that those who attempt suicide when help is readily available *are* doing it right, since their ambivalence is still in the forefront. They're not leaping into death with both feet, but keeping one foot in each camp. That's normal.

He couldn't hear me, though. I could tell. I got one of those looks that said, "Oh God, that's right. I forgot she was one of those bleeding-heart shrinks." Well, he was partially right. My heart *was* bleeding. It was, however, intact enough to resent the hell out of him and to lead my brain to generate two sarcastic thoughts. One was, "My son would get his stamp of approval," and the other was a reminder not to "cast ye your pearls before swine." It takes energy to educate the ignorant. I was fresh out. I didn't even have the energy to embarrass him.

I'm equally exasperated by people who say they don't have the "courage" to commit suicide. To survive the suicide of someone you love is to understand irrevocably that, in nearly every case, it is an act of cowardice. We talk of the fever pitch of the moment of self-destruction—pulling the trigger, jumping from the chair, washing down the pills—as though it were a definitive act of will. In doing so, we lose sight of the fact that it represents a complete *failure* of will.

The will to go on. The will to keep trying. The will to do one's best with whatever one was given.

That, far more than my inevitable failures as a parent, is what I'm ashamed of. The fact that my son was a coward.

# SIX

# Survivorship

As I SAID, THANKSGIVING CAME despite the fact I didn't feel thankful. It's backing up a little in the story, but I want to tell you what I wrote in my journal that Thanksgiving Day, 1984.

> I work (my "pen slipped")
>
> I woke up this morning and, as every morning, I cried. This morning though, there were a few minutes before it started, minutes in which I was surprised to think, "I'm not crying yet. I wonder if I'm not going to do it." I was only curious.
>
> Then, I began to think again—about the litany of sins and omissions against him—about how he would have been justified in blaming me and wondering if, in those last tormented moments, he did.
>
> And then I began to remember my last near brush with suicide. Not the first, perhaps not the last, but that time nine years ago when my drive or will or whatever you call it, almost got used up and me along with it.
>
> I remember how I planned it—every detail—ensuring that I *would* die. In my head, I composed notes to those two people I could still remember loving.
>
> And the point is, I didn't blame anybody but myself. It wasn't forgiveness—it was just that they were irrele-

vant. I wanted to cease existing, I wanted to erase myself, I wanted to have never *been*. I looked back over my life and I saw only *my* mistakes. And I told myself that love was an illusion or that, if it existed, *I* could not find it or something bad inside me saw to it that I could not keep it.

I talked to my friends, the main one being Tom. I talked to my family, mostly Jim and Peggy. And I said nothing of the suicidal thoughts. I said I was "down." I said I was "depressed." I catalogued my injuries at the hands of others in endless, repetitive detail, but the real feeling behind that was self-loathing, not blame. I knew many people were "there for me" and that all I had to do was ask and they'd swoop me up in their arms and save me from myself.

But I didn't ask. At least not that I know of, though I suspect Tom heard something inside me coming loose the clearest. Maybe he pulled me back from the edge, telling me it was great that I *understood* all this, but what was I going to *do* about it? It gave me the kick in the seat of the pants I needed to go for some help. Nonetheless, I believe I came back only because part of me didn't want to jump.

My "brakes" were Jim and Peggy—or so I thought. I would imagine their devastated faces and imagine their self-accusations and I could not bear it—the guilt of doing that to them outweighed my desire to obliterate myself.

And that led me to conclude that there must be such a thing as love—I love therefore love exists. And if I had the capacity to love them, then life could be endured— even if I never had anyone else.

I am only now becoming aware of how much of me has always wanted to exist. Maybe I found what I did and fastened onto it only because there is a part of me that loves me. And maybe that exists for each of us—including my Jim. But you hold on or you let go—sometimes deciding in a split second. I think it's why he chose the method he did—part of him knew he wanted to and deserved to live, but part of him believed the opposite and he wanted that side to be stronger.

He said, "I must have the courage to protect the ones I love," and he left us some loopholes to interpret that with. I think he meant to protect us, most of all me, from the badness inside himself. The tragedy is that it, like *my* badness, was so illusory. Such a small percentage.

I sound as though I had this all figured out, don't I? Believe me, I didn't. I'm just used to overfunctioning, as I said. Throughout my life, I've given the impression I'm confident and impervious to those things that knock mere mortals to their knees. As a friend likes to put it, I've got a bad case of thinking I'm Superwoman.

I had symptoms of the three great plagues which typically strike survivors: depression (half or more of us); post-traumatic stress disorder; and psychosomatic illness. For me, the psychosomatic component (which, may I remind you, is not "in the head," but *caused* by the head—or an immune system impaired by grief) was a sudden worsening of chronic back pain. I'd had a herniated lumbar disk in January of 1983 and had spent a week flat on my back, taking muscle relaxants and anti-inflammatory agents in an effort to avoid a myleogram (an X-ray involving a spinal tap) and subsequent back surgery. The conservative treatment had more or less worked—more, because I did avoid those things; less, because for the next few years I never had a waking moment without some pain in my lower back. That was still the case when Jim died and my pain cranked up to the screaming-meemie level.

I don't know if this will make any sense to you, but that was okay with me. Part of it was a masochistic need to suffer, but another part of it was the vindication I felt, bearing something Jim found unbearable. I needed to be reassured of my own strength, and the back pain performed that function admirably.

I knew that my depressive symptoms—things like confusion, fatigue, frequent crying, disturbed sleep, and decreased appetite—are so natural to acute grief that they're not considered "pathological." Nor does a person typically need to take antidepressants for them. Along with those symptoms, I had a profound sense of worthlessness, but knowing it went with the territory, I didn't worry a whole lot about it either.

When I thought it over, I decided that, if I wanted to go on functioning (which I did), I needed to sleep—and if I wanted to sleep, I was going to have to take sleeping pills in order to do it. I know their limitations and hazards, so I determined I would do that for one month, then stop taking them, even if it meant I didn't sleep for several nights because of the "rebound" dreaming I knew they would probably cause. I *was* methodical about that. I made a deal with myself and I stuck to it. The reason is very simple. I understand that drug abuse (whether of prescription drugs, street drugs, or alcohol) is simply a form of suicide. It's slower and less certain than Jim's method, but it's what suicidologists call "parasuicide"—meaning it is suicide's next-door neighbor. I had already made up my mind I wasn't going to be part of these statistics: there is an 80–300 percent greater chance of suicide among survivors and over a third of families will have more than one suicide among their members.* Having decided that I wasn't going to go whole-hog, I sure as hell wasn't going to do it halfway. As I said earlier, my son got his "if you're gonna do it, do it all the way" streak from me. A curse in his case, a blessing in mine.

I mentioned post-traumatic stress disorder. That's a set of symptoms most often associated with Vietnam vets. It certainly

*Christopher Lukas and Henry M. Seiden, *Silent Grief: Living in the Wake of Suicide* (New York: Scribners, 1987).

isn't confined to them, though. I've seen it in survivors of automobile accidents, incest survivors, other suicide survivors, and myself. The scenario is that something catastrophic takes place and repercussions rain down for years, impairing the survivor's ability to function fully in the here and now. My profession (and the media) has a tendency to focus on the more spectacular symptoms such as nightmares, flashbacks, or avoidance of anything that reminds the person of the triggering event(s). However, equal devastation can come from a blunting process in which parts of the self get walled off in an effort to protect them. The person can become a kind of emotional zombie or have a crazy sense of not knowing who they are. "How do you feel about that?" becomes a loaded question. A female in our culture will generally look baffled or try to answer, based on what she thinks the person asking wants. An American male will usually stonewall. "I don't have *any* feelings about that," or a shrug is his response.

I went down the middle. I had nightmares, still can't bear to watch the motions leading up to someone shooting himself (in a movie), and have gone on persistent sorties so I could get in there and knock down the walls I erected around some of my most painful emotions. Because I know I *need* those feelings. They are part of the whole and I am not my true self without them.

But there were times those walls meant I couldn't give a good answer to my friends' questions, times when I said, "Yes, I feel terrible," because I knew they expected me to feel terrible and, since I didn't at that moment, I assumed I was kidding myself. Other times, I couldn't even summon the energy to check where I was and I'd mumble, "I'm okay," shutting off any further questions/concern.

Or, to give you a different illustration, I saw a woman the other day who maintains a perpetual smile. Her life is a complete mess and she has not one clue how it came about. When I asked her which of her problems she thought we needed to tackle first, she answered, "I need to figure out what love is and how to know when it's the real thing." Not to make light of that, but it's hardly good problem solving. I see this person as being up to her neck in quicksand and, understanding it's an emergency, I start scrambling around, frantically looking for rope or a branch, only to be told, "Forget that. I'd rather you just relax, so we can have a nice chat about the Meaning of Life." When I see that kind of disconnectedness (and the person's not psychotic), I assume post-traumatic stress disorder until proven otherwise.

Working on gaining access to our feelings is another way of expressing our commitment to live. It says that we won't be partial people. We won't settle for going through the motions. Nor will we be satisfied with huddling in a corner indefinitely. Maybe we need to do it for a while, but there comes a time when continuing to do so represents a kind of death.

There are other ways we express our commitment to live: general, commonsense ways and uniquely individual ways. About three months after Jim died, I began to exercise regularly, to change my diet (higher fiber, lower fat), and to use some self-hypnosis techniques I'd learned years before in order to lower my stress level. The self-hypnosis techniques also had an added perk of offering me a way to "dialogue" with myself.

All relaxation techniques derive from our awareness that we need to replenish ourselves sometimes and that there is, within each of us, a calming, steadying force which is our ally and which offers us a sense of connectedness with the universal. While I'm in a trance-state, I summon what's referred to as an "inner guide"—a figure who represents the loving and wise aspects of myself. The idea is to make those things more available to me, to, in a sense, ask my own advice (and who knows me better?) about what I need to pay more attention to or how I might look at something differently.

When I first started doing it, I conjured up a Merlin-like figure, complete with beard and flowing robes. He was very impressive. Then, out of the blue, Arnold Schwarzenegger showed up. I was a bit taken aback, but believing as I do in the wisdom of the unconscious, I left the image alone. I can't tell you what fast friends we became. He's good-natured and gentle, a straight-shooter who gives me his blessing if what I need and want to do is tear my hair out for a while. But, as he put it once, "Just be aware it doesn't help your son." It's good to know the difference between doing penance and actual atonement. (Simply put, in both cases, you feel guilty. In the first, you do something to punish yourself. In the second, you do something to set things right with whomever/whatever you've wronged.) I think the reason I conjured up Arnold was that I needed his muscles to exemplify the principle that gentleness, good humor, and letting go of guilt are manifestations of strength. I'm very grateful to him for supplying an attractive wrapper for those ideas.

He wasn't the only odd expression of my self-caretaking. Another one was my braces. For ten or fifteen years, various dentists had nagged me about getting them. The standard wisecrack was, "Your teeth are great, Sue, but your gums have gotta go." I had chronic gum infections because my teeth were so crooked that I couldn't keep food out of the spaces between them. (That's not strictly true—I could have flossed every time I put a bite in my mouth. But, poo on that!)

About the time I started my other measures, I surrendered and asked for a referral to an orthodontist who worked with adults. Pretty soon, there I sat in the waiting room, about to turn forty-three—just me and the other pubescent folks—thinking bizarre thoughts like, "This is a commitment to live three more years." Know where I got that? It came from my inability to imagine being buried with braces. I know how strange that sounds, but what can I tell you? It's what I thought.

If you haven't gone through the ordeal, let me tell you. Braces are miserable. It's like having a truck parked in your mouth. Every time you have them adjusted, you feel like you've been beaten to a pulp. I kept telling my orthodontist that if my modeling career didn't pay off, I was going to come back and wreak my vengeance upon him. He laughed a lot, which was, of course, easy enough for him. It did me some good, though. It cheers me up to cheer people up; this was especially so during that first year.

Eventually, my energy increased, my outlook improved. Finally, a day came, some nine or ten months after my son died, when I began to feel well enough to "minister" to others. I wrote an article on surviving suicide that was ultimately published in the *Bulletin of the Menninger Clinic.* In it, I tried to inform therapists about this special type of bereavement, hoping a better understanding would enable them to be more helpful to survivors.

Then I looked around me and wondered what else I could do in the words of Isaiah, to "give unto them beauty for ashes, the oil of joy for mourning," and I hit on the idea of working with cancer patients. Compassionate Friends, the support group for bereaved parents, was dear to my heart but much too close to home. I felt that, if I wanted to be effective, I needed a little distance between my suffering and that of the people I was trying to help.

Cancer patients were a logical choice for me because I'd done extra training in hypnosis and geriatrics during the fourth year of my residency. Because of my work with the elderly, I had developed a certain level of comfort in dealing with death and dying, as well as with the reality that not everything is "fixable." In addition, hypnosis led me to believe that our state of mind is influenced by positive suggestion. That, coupled with exposure to some of the fascinating work done with biofeedback and guided imagery at Menninger, set the stage for a method based on the work of Carl and Stephanie Simonton.

In their book, *Getting Well Again,* they outlined a program for self-healing which, lo and behold, emphasized relaxation/ mental imagery, exercise, diet, and a host of mental exercises designed first to acknowledge and then to change those aspects of oneself that perpetuate illness. It's hard even now to describe the moment when I realized that I'd followed their program without knowing about it—that my inner physician had given me the same prescriptions they gave their patients.

There is a kind of basic practicality to the Simonton program, but I'd like to tell you why I think I stumbled onto them. I think there is a basic premise from which we all operate, whether we articulate it or not. That is, we see the universe as either benign or malevolent. Everything we do arises from which assumption we make. If our expectations are based on the belief that life's out to get us, we'll see injury and defeat around every corner. If, on the other hand, we trust in the benignancy of the universe, we will brave the darkest nights of our lives, believing that there are forces within and without us which will always enable us to not only endure, but sometimes transcend. It's the kind of trust illustrated by Guillaume Apollinaire when he wrote:

> Come to the edge
> No, we will fall
>
> Come to the edge
> No, we will fall
>
> They came to the edge
> He pushed them, and they flew

I believe we're capable of flying—that, in fact, soaring is a far more "natural" activity for the soul than occupying itself with safety and insurance against disaster. Because I believe this, I'll do whatever I can to provide a proper runway. That means taking care of myself, whether that's in a physical or psychological sense—and the Simonton methods are a clearly organized and easily understood way to do that.

The bottom line of all my talk about working with cancer patients or doing something else to reach out to others is that altruism is a good way of taking care of ourselves. It's a path many survivors go down, perhaps the preferred path for those who sur-

vive with the greatest sense of intactness and who know that, as
Rod McKuen said once, "Love at best is giving what you need to
get."

We help ourselves in the act of helping others.

# SEVEN

# Whence Help Comes

I'VE CERTAINLY BEEN the recipient of help. I looked back at my journal and found an entry dated December 13, 1984:

> I talked to a friend last night. We met about 15 years ago in college and, though we seldom see each other, our contacts are never superficial. She knew Jim and me together and she knows me pretty well, so she drew the logical conclusion that I'm being rough on myself. She had made a reservation to fly here and talk to me, but I had a conflict both in scheduling and in need so I called to talk instead.
>
> She said things a part of me knows—the part that will eventually heal me. They were things my family had said, but which came from a different angle and were thereby meaningful in a different way. "You did your best." "You're so damn introspective and willing to heap guilt on yourself." "Anyone could see how special your relationship was." "He was an adult—you hope for the best, you do your best, but you can't control your child's life—it doesn't belong to you."
>
> In a strange way, what helps me is the feeling of

specialness my friends and family give me, combined
with the things they say that give my experience a certain
commonality. It's the paradox that drives my work. To
patients, I say in attitude or words, "You are unique. You
are special. There is no one who has lived your life or
experienced exactly what you have experienced. But your
suffering is common. Many people have had the same
feelings, the same problems, the same illnesses. Many
people have said to themselves the same thing you're saying to yourself. I'll do my best to understand you. I'll give
you the benefit of my training and experience. I'll care
what happens to you and I'll hope even when you don't.
I'll loan you my strength, my humor, my seriousness—
anything I've got for as long as it *truly* helps you—you've
got it."

It's an imperfect statement, made by an imperfect
person. And sometimes I fall down, sometimes I'm distracted, sometimes I'm impatient, sometimes I weaken
people with my compassion, sometimes I ask too much
too fast. But I do the best I can with what I've got and
with what I know. I have to believe I didn't do any less
with my Jim.

Some of the other entries around that same time read:

12–15–84    Another thing to be grateful for—if there's
a nuclear war, I've got less to lose.

As in all the big events of life, this one's got mile-
stones (or do I mean millstones?). Yesterday was four
weeks, tomorrow is one month.

I try to evaluate if I'm any "better" and the answer
that comes back to me is "maybe a little quieter." I felt
this crazed woman inside me. It was an image of a woman
alone in the middle of a prairie, dress torn (no, *rent,* like
my life), her hair all awry, no grace in her movements as

she lurches along, shrieking at God and Fate and her parents and herself. Tears that won't come and thus scald her more.

She still exists inside me—she just occupies a little less space.

Tom wants to be cremated so I've told him and my family that I wish to be buried next to Jim. I'm buying that plot. It's interesting how Jim's death makes my own conceivable.

And I've decided on my epitaph. Jim's says, "Beloved Son." I gave it to him and he gave mine to me. It will say, "Jim's Just All Right Mother."

I can't remember the year, but know he was somewhere between eleven and fourteen. It was Mother's Day and he gave me a plastic statuette. It's a dowdy-looking little woman with a pleasant smile on her face and it looks like she's stirring a batch of cookies. On the front of the statue, it says, "World's Best Mother."

I was so pleased and flattered. I turned to him and asked, "Aw, Jim, do you really think so?"

His eyes twinkling, a grin on his face, he shrugged and answered, "Nah. They just didn't have one that said, 'World's Just All Right Mother.' "

Who am I to disbelieve my son? His death was his choice and not necessarily a condemnation of me. He told me I was a just all right mother in so many ways, so many times. He judged me good enough, always with more charity than I would show myself. And maybe it's the height of conceit to hold onto my guilt. Maybe to do so is to usurp his authority and rob him of his dignity and meaning.

I don't know why he died. But, then again, I don't know why he lived.

I'm just glad he did.

I think about the Tennessee Williams character who said, "I depend on the kindness of strangers." I guess I hold a different point of view—to me, if people are kind, they are no longer strangers.

So many people are kind to me—so many draw it from me—so many all unknowing.

My patients have been kind to me. Perhaps they sense something. I go on "like before," say so many of the same things, but they seem to speak softer, to be more candid, to share a greater part in unraveling the mysteries that make up their lives.

I don't trust myself to say I'm a better therapist. It seems to be so, but I can't judge.

It's so hard to say what my work means to me right now. My mother said, "It takes your mind off things," and I answered, "No, if anything, it focuses my mind *on* Jim." Yet, I'm aware that my role makes it easier. They don't know of my loss, so I'm not a grieving mother—I am the doctor—and their expectations of me make me oscillate less. But I'm still me and I've never been *just* my role.

Have you ever been in a crowded place and you had a headache, but didn't have any aspirin? You looked around until you saw someone who looked like—you just *knew* from looking at her—she'd have aspirin in her purse and she'd give you some if you asked? Well, that lady was me. I've joked about how many times that's happened to me—and the fact that, yes, I did have the aspirin, and yes, I did give it to them.

I've also joked that I'm eminently qualified to be a shrink since I've *had* every problem anyone could come to me with. Well, not quite, but I've had enough to develop "coping skills."

Still, it makes me very angry to hear the old saw about

people in psychiatry/psychology who are "trying to work out their own problems with their patients." I don't need my patients for that and I don't think the majority of my colleagues do either. We may grow within the context of helping others, but that doesn't mean we were incomplete without them.

Someone well-qualified to evaluate me once said, "You have a history of deciding what you want and pursuing it until you get it." It's no accident that I am now getting letters and messages of love and support from friends. It's no accident that I have exactly the husband I want and need. It's no accident that I am doing work that I love and doing it well.

I don't know why I persevere and Jim couldn't. I understand his despair, his impulse to self-destruct—I've been so close myself. I think the difference between us is either slight or tremendous—maybe both—but I'm not sure what it is.

My mother is an interesting woman and sometimes I wish I knew her. She gave me my brains (this nasty voice just said, "She could afford to—she wasn't using them"). She also gave me a sense of justice and a penchant for irony. When I was a kid, we saw some other kids taunting a black child. My mother stopped the car, chased the tormentors off, comforted the black child, got back in the car, and drove off, lecturing my brother and me on the fact that, if she ever caught us treating another human being in such a shabby, cruel way, she'd beat us within an inch of our lives.

She played with us. Tickled us and laughed and got us a dumb dog that we loved. She gave me endless spelling quizzes, always helped with homework when asked, made my costumes for dance recitals, always came to them,

finagled clothes and a generous allowance out of my tigh-
twad Dad, hit on the perfect solution for brother-sister
wars ("If you don't quit fighting, I'll make you kiss each
other"), remembered cute things I'd said or done, read
constantly, thus improving my vocabulary with her own
enriched one. She gave me a certain "presence" and the
belief that women are supposed to have it. It stuck more
because she verbalized the opposite and believes she is the
opposite. Both she and my father think she's the dependent one, he's the strong one. Well, maybe that's their
"deal"—the bargain they struck 50 years ago when she
was the brightest fifteen year old on the horizon and he
was the handsome strong man of 22. Maybe for them it's
true—maybe she's still that delicate slip of a girl leaning
on his arm, maybe he's still that square-jawed, determined young man.

How should I know? I only know what I wish they
had been. It's hard to let them just be people. But that's
really all they are. That's really all I am. I'm not a monster
who drove my son to suicide any more than they are
monsters who nearly drove me to it. I nearly drove myself.
I made the choice to live and it was my choice to make.
Just as all the other choices of my life (including clinging
to my resentment) have been mine to make. Just as Jim's
were his to make.

I loved my son.

I love my son.

I will always love my son.

Sometimes I'm aware that past, present, and future
don't exist—that they're only conveniences we invented
to make life a little more comprehensible, a little more
manageable. I wish I could get by without it, that I could
move unencumbered by time and see Whitman's "calm
and actual faces," Jim's among them, that surround me
and blend with me.

Thought for the day: Grief means always making sure you have on waterproof mascara.

In my journal, I copied some letters from friends along with my answers to them. Here is a response dated December 16, 1984:

"I wanted to thank you for your letter—for the understanding and concern it conveyed—for sharing your own loss with me—for sharing the hope that my own 'hearing' will be deeper and richer for having gone through my own tragedy. I feel that it is already, but I don't trust myself or my ability to assess that right now. It would be too comforting a 'reason' for Jim's death and I need to exhaust all the possibilities and live with the chaos for a while.

"I do have a husband who comforts me—sometimes by leaving me alone, sometimes by talking with me, sometimes by just holding me. His relationship with Jim was based on proximity to me—they were friendly strangers, yet he knew Jim in an objective way and liked what he saw. The fact that he didn't love him helps me. The fact that my family did love him helps me.

"My co-workers talk to me if I open the subject and don't if I don't. That helps me too.

"Poetry helps me. Writing helps me. Crying helps me. Sleeping pills on work nights help me. Being unable to sleep on weekends helps me. Remembering Jim's life instead of his death helps me. Friends like you help me. My belief that time will help helps me. Laughter helps me. Television helps me. Asking people for favors and realizing they're relieved to be able to do something for me helps me. Helping my patients helps me. Saying 'Ask so-and-so, I'm not up to handling the problem right now' helps me. Just walking out if I hit my limit helps me. My patients' not knowing helps me. Wallowing in my guilt from time to time helps me. Knowing that I felt guilty before helps me. Others' expectations of me help me. Getting angry at their expectations helps me. Not having to cook helps me. Talking to my brother and sister helps me.

"I'd give anything to have Jim back—but there's nobody to make that deal with. It's the most painful loss of my life, but I've had other losses, devastating to me at the time, and I've survived them. I know I'll survive this— sometimes I don't see how and sometimes a part of me doesn't much care—but I know I will.

"Thank you for caring."

**12–16–84**   There is no way Jim could have doubted my love for him. What's battering my heart to bits are my doubts about his love for me. I reason and I reason and I reason, but I can't factor out my own pain. I can't say, "I understand, Jim. I know you didn't do this to me in order to do this to me." I suppose that's anger, but that seems to be a cleaner, less complex emotion than what I feel. Anger feels like fire—this feels like lead or a bloody, surreptitious sacrifice, shamefully done, the weight of it on my soul. It's bitterness and malice and anguish admixed with all the above. It's a question slamming into walls, a cosmic "Why?" that will never be answered, like one of Kafka's nightmare scenes.

**12–17–84**   Writing in my journal is a catharsis. Sometimes I think the words may etch their way down through layers of paper, they're so full of pain and anger, but so far they stay put. Or maybe they're burning their way through unknown layers of unknown things.

**12–18–84**   The sum of our offenses was exceeded by the total of Jim's misery. Which means he added something to the equation.

We all take some vipers to our bosom. We all nourish certain slights or offenses. We all fail ourselves—some ways, some times. We all have things we can't forgive in ourselves or others.

Jim made a drastic decision, but he acted on impulses we all have.

Sometimes I understand why he did it the way he did. There's the ironic thoughtfulness of not having one of us find him. And there's the total, final commitment to substitute for the smaller ones (or do I mean the larger ones?) he couldn't make.

There's the desire to take control, to decide one's fate, to "finally do something right." The fact that those things seem wrongly reasoned doesn't make them false in Jim's mind at the time he thought them.

**12–19–84**    I know that nobody helps me with my grief more than me. That's lonely at times, but it's also reassuring—because I've always *got* me. I don't have to count on capricious fate—I don't have to wait around to see if I've been good enough for God or Santa Claus to come.

Many things/people help, many don't—I like being the one to decide. I value those decisions, even if sometimes I make the wrong one, knowingly or unknowingly. Jim had that right—everybody does.

I can't say I've made my peace with his decision. How can I, when a part of that decision involved inflicting pain on me? That factor was outweighed by other things in Jim's mind, but it's the heaviest element in mine. Part of him knew the agony I'd feel. That fact rattles my teeth and the best I can hope for is that I'll learn to co-exist with it.

**12–20–84**    His expectations of himself always exceeded his reality. We all tried to say to him in every way it could be said, "Jim, we think you're great. You are bright. You are capable. You are special." But he wouldn't or couldn't believe it.

So many people are satisfied with so much less than Jim had. Every day kids go forth on their own—afraid or unafraid. Why couldn't he?

I know about self-doubt, how corrosive it is, but I don't understand why his was so overwhelming. I know how you get out on the ledge—I just don't know how you jump.

**12–22–84**   My associate, Ken, asked me if I was going to a Christmas party. I said, "No, I don't feel too sociable right now." Our friendship's good enough for him to laugh and ask, "How can you tell the difference?" (My dislike of parties is legendary.)

He likes to kid me. He referred a patient to me once. It turned out very well and he said, "I just knew if she could work with a mature, strong, but feminine woman, she'd do well." I was composing my thank you, just the right trace of modesty in it, when he added with a grin, "But *you* were available."

I really did feel the punchline coming. I was still impressed—I am not easy to outwit.

**12–24–84**   God, I had a miserable night last night. I guess I slept about four hours. Some of that sleeplessness was caused by a nurse calling me at 2:30 A.M. to ask about giving a patient a second sleeping pill. (I felt like laughing hysterically and shouting, "Sure! God forbid anybody should have a sleepless night!"). The real problem, though, was that I kept doing all these "if onlies." Thinking of every conceivable action or reaction at every conceivable point where it might have mattered.

I hate it being Christmas without him. I hate time rolling on in its inexorable way and the goddamn world looking so *normal.* I hate having people wish me Merry

Christmas and having to respond with a smile, however wan, and say, "You too."

In two days it will be a year since I last saw him, alive and laughing. My Jimmo, Jimbo, Jimmy, Jim. My baby, boy, man son. Oh what a hateful, hateful world I'm in right now. A world without that radiant smile, a world without that infectious laugh, a world without someone so loved who calls me Mom. I see his face in so many other young men, but not *his* face, not truly my Jim.

How can it be?

How can he have been taken from my body—now from my life?

I had so little to do with his everyday life—he so little to do with mine. How can it be that his death leaves such a gaping hole, such an abyss?

400 miles separated us. What separates us now? I don't really know—just that I can't bridge it.

Forsaken. Forlorn. Forbearance.

The Lord is my shepherd, I shall not want. . . . Surely goodness and mercy shall follow me all the days of my life. . . .

Mercy is in the eye of the beholder. Mercy would have been a plane crash on the way home—the only time in my life I didn't give a shit at the thought.

The quality of mercy is not strained; it droppeth as the gentle rain from Heaven.

Really? I thought it was shit. That's what it feels like at this moment—like the heavens opened up with a great thunderclap (a shot?)—and it's raining shit.

Merry Christmas! Merry Christmas! Ho Ho Ho!

Dasher, Dancer, Prancer, Vixen, Comet, Cupid, Donner, Blitzen. And, of course, don't forget Rudolph. May be foggy out tonight. (There's a shitstorm comin'.)

Gonna find out who's naughty or nice.

# EIGHT

# Widening Communication

FOR ME, COMMUNICATION lies at the heart of healing. We simply do not exist in a vacuum and, when our lives are blasted by tragedy, virtually none of us can contain all the shrapnel. Some flies out of us and hits those around us, some embeds itself near the surface and needs a little picking-at for extraction, some stays deep within us—of that, some can be gotten at with surgery and some will just have to be lived with because it's too close to a vital organ to be removed safely. We need the help of others either to take the necessary action or to bear with what we must.

I have a quirk when it comes to communication. I sometimes find it far easier to communicate profound thoughts and feelings in writing. Spoken words often fail me and I get frustrated when I start to cry. It feels as though the water filling my eyes short-circuits my brain. I don't *think* I'm ashamed of crying. I think I just prefer to talk when I talk and cry when I cry. Ne'er the twain shall meet. . . .

However, I can cry when I write. Doesn't interfere in the least. I spent hours and hours writing that journal after Jim died and cried buckets during most of it. Tom understood that it was therapy and blessedly left me to it. Then again, he knew I'd come to him for comforting when I needed it. We'd long since passed the point of having to say "Hold me" out loud.

I realized years before that I had some talent as a writer (though I still find it impossible to quantify). People told me that in high school, in response to letters, in college, in residency. I spent a number of years as a service wife, then moved around with schools and training. That means a lot of friends have come and gone, visiting my life as I've visited theirs. I've always tried to be there in my letters, to write in a way that makes the reader feel he or she has just had a good visit with me.

That carried over into other forms of writing. Although medical and psychiatric journals have certain rules and require the writer to follow a particular format, I found that, even working within their confines, I could still express a viewpoint that was uniquely my own. I entered an essay contest before Jim died and was notified the following January that I'd won and was to read my paper to the American Academy of Psychoanalysis in May. That gave me the confidence to enter another essay contest a year later and I won that one also, leading me to become a monthly columnist for a paper called *The Psychiatric Times* in July of 1986. My column has always been plainspoken, but over the years it has more and more become a letter to friends—a letter in which I've shared Jim's death and the thoughts, feelings, and experiences of a human being who is also, as it happens, a psychiatrist.

I've gotten enormous, mostly gratifying feedback from my readers and verified (was there ever any doubt?) that most of us are among the walking wounded. It's been important for me to say what I've said in the column and in answer to readers who've either written or talked to me at conferences. It's been equally important hearing what they said in response. Each is unique, but the common phrases (which mean everything) are, "You understand," and, "You helped."

Think about the tribute those contain. Then think about how

irrevocably the suicide cuts himself off from that kind of inter-change. Suicidology expert Edwin Shneidman has made the point that suicide notes don't make sense for the simple reason that if the suicide could effectively communicate what he's feeling he wouldn't need to kill himself. Shneidman also says that the suicide has renounced all possibility of help from the survivors. That kind of "cutoff," that circumventing of the communication process and possible understanding and help, was fatal to the suicide. It can be no less deadly to survivors. That's why they need to talk to those around them and to consider personal therapy or support groups like Survivors of Suicide and Compassionate Friends.

Do I need to say that it doesn't matter how articulate you are, how much education you have, how well you string your thoughts together? What matters is the effort to reach out to others, to exchange information for support and support for information. In trying to describe how to write dialogue, I once told a friend, "Think of it as a tennis match. The game is not in one swing; it's in the back and forth connections each person makes. Whack! The ball's in one person's court. Whack! It's in the other's."

Being a writer has only meant that I could communicate with more people. I can say that Jim's rejection of my help and under-standing made me feel worthless. I can say that, guilt for honest mistakes notwithstanding, it finally dawned on me that survivors are victims rather than murderers. In the first shock waves, that's what survivors are inclined to feel like—murderers. I did this, they tell themselves. This is my fault, they cry.

Well, let me give you Webster's definition of a *victim:* "Someone or something killed, destroyed, injured, or otherwise harmed by, or suffering from, some act, condition, agency, or circumstance."

Sounds like me all right.

How about you?

# NINE

# The"Why?" Conundrum

I NEED TO GO ON ONE OF MY TEARS and I hope you'll bear with me. It concerns one of those common-as-dirt misconceptions that inevitably leads us on a wild goose chase. It is that the *why* of any suicide is found in the particular. People ask me if I understand why Jim killed himself. Can I come up with a rationale for why a unique individual named Jim Scott killed himself, based on what I know of his circumstances and feelings? List the factors, they mean, so they can check off the things that don't pertain to them and thus feel less vulnerable.

Well, I can't do that because (a) it would be dishonest, given what I really think about causality, (b) it would invade Jim's privacy more than I'm willing to, and (c) it misses the point, which is that anybody who commits suicide does it because he can't see any other way to solve his problems. If I offered the list some people ask for, I'd be saying the problems are the cause. But guess what? Everybody has problems. All that was unique about Jim's was the way he let them pile up, doing nothing about them until they overwhelmed him.

You don't believe me? Think about it. Why does the terminal

cancer patient kill himself? Because he can't solve the problems of suffering unrelenting pain, depleting his family's resources, or growing increasingly helpless. Why does the samurai commit hari-kari? Because it's the only acceptable solution to a loss of face. Why does the financially ruined stockbroker dive out the window? Because he can't resolve the discrepancy between who he's been and who he's going to become. Why does the adolescent shoot himself when his girlfriend tells him it's over? Because he doesn't feel up to the task of dealing with his first major loss.

In each case, an observer might list the reasons: pain, becoming a burden, loss of reputation, reversal of finances, loss of love. This observer would see the forest but not the trees. Suicide is a statement that the person wants out of what he views as an insoluble dilemma. The tragedy is that virtually every dilemma has a solution. As some wag once put it, suicide is a permanent solution to a temporary problem.

I've already mentioned the kick in the seat of the pants Tom gave me when we were friends rather than lovers or mates. I was bemoaning my problems when, after a long pause, he said, "I think it's great the way you've figured all this out, the insight you have, the analysis you've done. What I want to know is what you're going to do about it."

His words infuriated me, and I didn't speak to him for several months. When I finally did, it was because his words had spurred me into seeking psychotherapy and getting some of my old garbage worked out. I saw that he was right, that it wasn't enough to beat my breast and enumerate the ways I'd been wronged. It was up to me to set some things right and get on with it. That was 1975. It turned out to be excellent training and a lesson in the fact that insight without action is fruitless. It's not enough simply to sit and mull things over, even if we're doing it correctly. We have to put our knowledge into action or we'll ride a closed loop that doubles endlessly back on itself.

As I've said before, sometimes that action is just communicat-

ing what we're thinking to another. Sometimes it's removing ourselves from an untenable situation. Sometimes it's seeking help
for things outside our control.

One of the most common things outside our control is depression. It's a broad term, signifying different things to different
people. There's the understandable and perfectly appropriate reaction to circumstances (such as bereavement) most of us mean
when we say the word. But there's also what my profession sometimes calls clinical depression, which is a whole different animal.
It is a biochemical imbalance in the brain which often leads to
inappropriate (sometimes baffling) reactions to ordinary circumstances. Seemingly out of nowhere a cloud descends and everything gets difficult and grim. Sleep eludes the person, moving
about becomes more and more tiresome, and concentration is
disrupted. With that come memory problems. The individual
gets anxious, wondering if he's faced with Alzheimer's or losing
his mind in some other, equally insidious way. Tears come frequently when they've been rare or unrelentingly when they've
been common. And whatever ailments the person's been subject
to just get worse. In Jim's case, backaches; in mine, headaches.

I know depression from several angles. Although I've never
taken medication for it, I know I've had it several times. I've had
friends with it and seen hundreds of patients with it. And I know
my son had it.

You know that old saying about leading a horse to water but
not being able to make him drink? I know on every level that it's
true. I told Jim I thought he was depressed, suggested he see
somebody about it. I know Peggy did the same. He blew us off,
plain and simple. During the times I've been depressed, I have
explained it away, making all my symptoms appear rational to me.
I remember being startled when, just before giving a speech on
depression, I ran down a little questionnaire I'd copied for the
audience and discovered that when I answered it on the basis of
how I'd felt six weeks before, my score showed "moderate depres-

sion." I recalled cheerily explaining to a friend that, yes, I had lost ten pounds, but it was because food didn't inspire me much those days, and no, I wasn't sleeping more than a few hours a night, but that was to be expected, given some of the changes I was going through, and hey, the fact that I cried so much I couldn't be fitted for contacts was perfectly understandable, given my circumstances.

Amazing, our capacity for self-delusion. . . .

I do not assume that, just because people are miserable enough to come to my office and pay my fee, they will actually believe me when I tell them they're depressed or that medication is likely to help them in two to four weeks. Some do wholeheartedly. But I know that others just figure they haven't had a better offer so they might as well humor me. After all, I seem like a nice person and I've got lots of nifty diplomas on the wall.

I ask about suicidal thinking, and if I get a yes, I ask about plans. If they have one, I ask if they have the means to carry it out. I've discovered a few people who are "rehearsing," putting a gun in their mouth or to their temple while they watch themselves in the mirror. I've had some who've accumulated enough pills to do the job. They know it and I know it. They scare the crap out of me and I generally tell them that plainly.

You want to hear something weird? The only two patients I've ever had kill themselves were women who both denied vociferously that they'd ever do such a thing. Both were burdened with excessive guilt and a complete inability/unwillingness to talk about it. The first came for only one appointment. The second canceled innumerable appointments and dismissed my concerns every time I brought them up. I think she came to see me because part of her wanted to live, but she sabotaged me and her therapy because a larger part of her wanted to die.

I can't balance those things for anybody else. Not Jim, not my patients. If they ask me, I can put my weight on the side of life, but I have no control over what's on the other end of the scales.

And I sure as hell can't make them ask me in the first place.

Time and again, I've expounded that idea to other therapists. Even very experienced psychiatrists get caught up in the idea that we "keep patients alive." Nobody keeps anybody but him or herself alive. I'll use whatever means I have to strengthen the side of someone that wants to live and grow and prosper. It's the only thing I have to offer against the side that wants to die and stagnate and decay. Our name for that balancing act is ambivalence; we also use it in talking about the simultaneous love and hate we feel for those we are closest to. We are ambivalent because, make no mistake about it, the source of our greatest pleasure is also the source of our greatest pain. If you don't believe me, ask yourself which wounds you more, the criticism of an enemy or the neglect of a friend?

Those who entertain suicidal thoughts also entertain ideas of salvation. Help them a few inches in the direction of that salvation and they're often saved. However, bear in mind that they will select the form of their redemption. There's nothing more futile than trying to come up with reasons why somebody else should want to live and nothing more helpful than getting that person to explain his or her own reasons. I recently had a patient who kept defeating everybody with her "I don't want to live and you can't make me" gambits. When she sprung it on me, I said, "You're right."

Looking startled, she said, "Huh?"

I answered, "You're right. I can't make you."

She eyed me suspiciously a moment or two, then explained that, having recently raked up the sexual abuse she'd suppressed for thirty years, she now found life intolerable and didn't see how she could go on.

I thought it over, then said, "Well, if I may point out, these things happened to you thirty years ago, yet you found it possible to go on back then. Why could you go on when the hurt was fresh, but can't now that it's rehashed hurt?" When she didn't answer, I added, "See, I could give you reasons all day, but they'd be *my* reasons for staying alive. I'd rather hear what your reasons were because they must have made sense to you back then and might still make sense to you now."

Suffice it to say, there were reasons and they did make sense.

# TEN

# The Petard of Ambivalence

A MOMENT AGO, I talked about ambivalence. I'd like to say something else about that, since I think it's the source of a lot of suffering for survivors.

When someone close to you has trouble—serious, chronic trouble—there is a part of you that grows very tired of that. You see your loved one struggle and struggle and struggle, and you see that he's never quite able to surmount whatever his obstacles are. You are discouraged and sometimes disgusted by that. You alternately bleed for him and feel like giving him a swift kick. Sometimes, your anger explodes. Other times, it's driven underground—sometimes so far that you even forget it was there.

Then, when and if your loved one commits suicide, all your negative feelings boomerang and come back to whack you upside the head. They tell you they are the reason your loved one died, that if you hadn't felt them, that son or daughter, husband or wife, would have found life so sweet there's no way he or she could have left it. And as if that weren't enough, somewhere inside you a voice will whisper, "I don't have to worry about him anymore," and you'll know a second of relief, then years of guilt because it seems like you were wishing your loved one dead.

It's the classic dilemma of the parent of a severely retarded child or the spouse of an Alzheimer's patient. There is love, often in abundance, but there is also weariness and never-ending grief for things that either never were or never will be again. When life finally ebbs away entirely, the survivor feels a crater where the absorption with the other's needs once was, and in the bottom of it he or she senses a small puddle of relief. Recognition of that puddle is intolerable to many, especially right after the loss. It is nonetheless there and it is perfectly understandable.

I watched Jim struggle unsuccessfully with many things and I worried about him a lot. I tried the means I knew to help, the means he'd let me try. Still, I couldn't do it for him, and I couldn't help being exasperated when he stayed stuck. All that's by way of saying that, yes, I did feel a fleeting sense of relief when it all ended, and yes, that was followed closely by guilt. But the truth is, I didn't cause him to default in order to relieve my anxieties about him; therefore my guilt is inappropriate. Maybe that realization wouldn't help everybody, but it helps me because it enables me to let go of it. I believe in keeping whatever guilt I deserve, but I refuse to keep that which I don't.

That's an odd way of putting it, I know. Still, the aftermath of suicide is so laden with guilt that you have to think of a way to sort it out and toss some of it in the "discard" bin if you hope to get on with your own life. You have to say from time to time, "Nope, that part doesn't belong to me," or you'll be overwhelmed by the sheer volume. It is, however, guaranteed that some of it will have your name on it. That's okay, since I'm assuming that your name isn't Jesus or Muhammad or Buddha. The rest of us, having imperfections aplenty, are bound to make mistakes for which we deserve to feel guilty. So be it.

I think I mentioned that my brother, David, consoled me one day with a simple, "You did the best you could with what you had and what you knew at the time." I think he was right—not that I think I did well, just that I neither had nor knew much at the times that were probably crucial for Jimbo/Jimmy. I don't know that I was particularly important to Jim, the young man. Most mothers probably have an exaggerated notion of their importance to their grown sons.

Another bit of ambivalence. When I read Jim's suicide note and realized later that no individual message was in the mail to me, I felt both slighted and relieved. Slighted because I hadn't been given the special consideration of such a message. Relieved because I hadn't been singled out as the decisive offender in his mind. Actually, his note only pointed the finger back at himself. He was going to do it to protect those he loved. David and my parents took that to mean he was involved in drugs and someone had threatened his family. I took it to mean his rage at my father would get the better of him and he'd kill Dad if he didn't kill himself first. I still lean in the direction of my theory. I don't question that Jim overused painkillers and drank too much sometimes. But I also know a lot about addicts and drug dealers (most of whom are addicts), and what I know doesn't fit Jim's profile. I admit I'm probably biased, both by my love for Jim and my own rage at my father, but I believe that's what his note meant nonetheless.

There is an interesting outgrowth of all this. When Jim died, I was, in a sense, cast adrift on the generational sea. Whether or not I was still a major consideration in his life, he was a major consideration in mine. A portion of my living was vicarious and done through him, just as I have always carried some baggage for my parents. When he left the world, all my energy came home to me. Simultaneously (though I didn't fully realize it until later), I checked my parents' luggage into a locker somewhere, as I lacked the strength or will to haul it around anymore.

Does that isolate me? You bet.

Does that free me? You bet.

Shortly after Jim died, I was hit by the realization that I'm all

I've got and that my actions from now on have to be based on fulfilling my own needs and desires. Most people losing their only child might be concerned about who is going to take care of them in old age. That's of some concern to me, but what I really mean about being cast adrift is that I can't draw any self-esteem or gratification from Jim's life anymore. It all has to come from my own.

That motivates me. That gives me a gigantic kick in the ass. It says I can forget flashing pictures of my good-looking son, his wife, and the grandkids as I talk about how they're prospering and growing. It says I'd better forget everything I've been thinking about safety and security and go for what pleases me and makes me feel real, because this moment is all I have. The future I was counting on has vaporized, and it's up to me to create a new one along the lines I'd like to see.

I have never, of course, been much for playing it safe. I did some of that when Jim was young and found it a soul-killing experience. Not that I'm an outlandish, iconoclastic heathen, contemptuous of the rules. It just that it's been a long time since I've been willing to pretend things are okay when they're not or stay when I knew I'd be happier going. It's amazing when you think of it—the amount of misery most people will live with in the name of stability. Since Jim's death, I can barely tolerate an ounce of it and sometimes it seems to me that most people are buried under tons.

Then again, I have resources and options a lot of people don't.

Beware of generalizations, she said with a smile.

# ELEVEN

# The Hunt for Stability

WE WERE TALKING ABOUT STABILITY, weren't we? Let me give you some more journal entries—ones which illustrate where I was headed, even that far back.

> 12–30–84    I married Jim's stepfather for certain illusions—stability and old-fashioned values being the main ones. And for years I told myself he'd fooled me. Then, for more years, I told myself I'd been the one to fool me. Finally, I arrived at what seems true to me.
>
> Stability—the only stability that counts—has to come from within. And if it isn't put there by consistent, loving parents, then it has to arrive in the face of a challenge to one's own integrity, one's own existence. It is the inner voice saying, "Though all crumbles about me, here I stand."
>
> As for old-fashioned values, there are fewer of those than I thought. There is only one thing that I think is always true. That is that cruelty is always wrong. Nothing is ever always right—especially not love, for it depends on

love of whom or what and there's always possessiveness attached to it, clinging to it like a parasite.

All of which means my reasons for marrying Hank were based on faulty logic. The things I sought in someone else were to be found within myself. And only if I found them in myself did they matter.

I can't live on someone else's strength—their roots, however deep, won't nourish me. My roots could not nourish Jim—and I think he perceived his own as too fragile. Maybe my father overshadowed his growth, eating up his sunlight. Maybe the soil I provided was lacking in some essential element. But it was all the soil I had to give him at the time. Too young soil, unenriched soil, soil newly ground from the hard and flinty mountain of my parents' childhoods and my own. I added what I could—perhaps too many flowers and not enough legumes. But I was unschooled in the ways of growing a son. I had only one chance and one bad example—another son, my brother, grown up like a weed, struggling for survival.

There are no oak trees in my family. It took a willow to survive. Or a hybrid like my brother, a combination of mesquite and prickly pear, enduring and difficult, stinging and yet tolerant of mistletoe, under which people kiss.

What was Jim? A maple maybe—full of untapped sweetness, but too hard to bend with life's gales.

It must be reading Robert Frost—my thinking of trees. But I also think of my brother-in-law, Lonnie. His father's name was Oak and I always wondered if he was one. I think Lonnie was, but it turned out to be the death of him. Because there are so few these days—and an isolated oak is a lightning rod—attracting its end to itself.

I still miss him—five and half years after his death. He had no experience of sisters, but he was a good brother to me. A grown man who didn't treat me like a brat though I probably was one. I wrote his eulogy and meant every word. I said nothing I hadn't already said when, ten years before, I had written a character sketch of him for a college English class. He was incredulous to find how much I admired him. He didn't know that his flaws didn't matter to me. I think they mattered more to Jim, but I also think Jim forgave and understood them, because they were largely self-inflicted flaws, like Jim's. You know, the kind that make you hurt yourself more than others— though you *do* hurt others in the process.

Peggy asked me to write the eulogy. I never questioned why. I thought it was because of that earlier, premature one or because the minister didn't know him or because she believed in my way with words and knew I would describe him with love. I know that it helped me. I know that it moved the others who loved him. It said:

"His father's name was Oak and it would have been a fitting name for him—for many of us have been sheltered by his strong branches and many of us have known the depth of his roots.

"He had only two children, one who came to him by birth and one who called him father because he loved her as one. And he had one brother, but who among us hasn't felt his brotherhood or known his love for children? He has made our children his and given them a share of specialness in knowing they each had a place in his large heart.

"He stood for many things, but perhaps most of all for a kind of quiet manhood that accepted the care and responsibility of others. He didn't label his ideals, he lived them, and he lived them unsparingly, always demanding more of himself than he would ever expect of others.

"His loss is keenest to those who loved him most, but it is shared by us all. For all of us have a special niche in

our hearts for him. It is a place he built himself with his
laughter, his friendship, and his love. It belongs to him
and he will always be there—living on in our hearts—
being there, strong and steadfast, for each and every one
of us as long as we shall live."

I remember twenty-year-old Jim putting his arm
around me, a sad and anxious look on his face, as the
eulogy was read at Lonnie's funeral. He was worried
about his Mom, he was being a man, comforting me.
I thought of that scene many times preparing for his
funeral—wishing it could be repeated, that I had found
words to eulogize my father and that Jim and I were
burying him instead.

**1–6–85**   I decided to try my hand at writing a haiku
here:

> The night mist envelops the
> slumbering flowers
> Their tears greet the dawn

It's like a gentle rain these days—you go about your
daily life and perhaps you notice, in a distracted or less-
than-attentive-way, that in the background there's a soft
pattering on the windowpanes, the sound of gurgling in
the gutters and drainpipes, a steady drip-drip-drip on the
porch, beating a cadence to some unknown song.

Jim is ever present, but blurred, then focused—too
sharply at times—blurred, then focused. I am startled by
the strings of moments I don't think of him. I am comfortable with echoes of him. I am torn asunder by the loss
of him.

Sometimes it catches me unawares—driving along in
my car, I begin to sob. No theme and therefore, no solution—just naked emotion, unlinked to conscious thought,
welling up and quenching the fires of reason and intellec-

tual understanding. Purpose, wisdom, strength—they're only the smoke from the spluttering flame. There is no warmth or light—only loss, loss, terrible in its might, crushing in its intensity—a total eclipse of the heart.

How do you put your son in the past? Worse yet, how do you fail to acknowledge that that's now where he is? I can only deny it so far. I can concentrate on immortality, oneness, reunion, but part of me knows that whomever I greet someday and however I greet him, it won't be the Jim he was before. It's such a simple thing—knowing you can pick up the phone and call—hear his voice, picture him sitting there, tapping his foot, draping himself over the chair.

**1-8-85**   I used to think catatonia looked attractive. It would be if it were like Ken Kesey's description of "the Chief's" gentle fog. I remember my dismay when I found out catatonia is really frozen will—the will to let anything in or out, for fear of doing the terrible things the mind brushes against in its inner excursions.

There's no such thing as a free lunch, right? No warm lavender fog . . . just slogging along, feeling music, smiling at children, reading poetry, getting angry, crying, remembering, planning, hoping, despairing, living. Most of all, living. Trying to love, wisely and well. Knowing that I can only try, only approximate. Giving myself permission. Trying to let that be enough. Trying to forgive myself. Trying to forgive Jim. Making myself stop tormenting myself when I reach the limits of my considerable endurance.

**1-13-85**   I had a very bad week. Not bad in an acute way, more a matter of running out of stores. I felt depressed in the gray sense, not the tearing my hair out sense. I had gray, disjointed dreams, all having to do with

Jim but never resolving or remembering what the point had been. The things I saw or clarified were all a blend of Jim's "pathology" and my culpability in either creating or failing to eradicate it.

I don't know if I was too self-absorbed, too involved with my own life. Right now I think I was. Right now I see only the missed opportunities to intervene—gone forever—gone forever. . . . I try to stop, to say to myself, "Stop torturing yourself. That's all you're doing. Jim didn't bequeath this pain, you're inflicting it on yourself."

He did what he did to end his suffering—not to begin mine.

It's so hard to stop.

Sometimes I just say, "Stop it! Stop it!" aloud or in my mind. Or if I'm starting to slide into one of my self-batterings, I make myself concentrate on something else. Then this doubt creeps in, "Oh, am I postponing it? Am I leaving unfinished business?" Well, I say, some business will never be finished and you don't pick a fight when you're in traction.

I got a letter from my mother about mid-week. She let me know that she'd given Jim's sleeping bag to my niece's stepson (as I'd agreed). She said, "Everyone has been pleased to get something of Jim's. Everyone liked Jim, he was always so pleasant to be around and he was always pleased to go to every family gathering and if there was a pretty unattached girl in the crowd, there's where Jim was. Oh, we loved him so much and miss him so much."

It was painful in its accuracy. There's always idealization after death, I suppose, but there's still the ring of truth in her words. Jim *was* always pleasant, everybody *did* like him. Even when he was a little boy, he made friends easily and had wonderful manners (despite the fact that he was also a little imp). His manners came from consideration, not drill, and held up even when I wasn't around to watch.

I wish he'd been nastier. I wish he'd punched my Dad's lights out. I wish he'd punched *my* lights out.

I guess he did. I just wish it hadn't cost him everything to finally do it. That he'd have found some way to do it and let *us* pay the price instead of him.

Instead. Look at the meaning. In someone else's stead. Did Jim die instead of me? Or was it instead of my father?

I know I expressed my wish that Jim had been there at the funeral—comforting me at my father's death. Is that a terrible thought? That I wish my father had died instead of my son? Well, I do. I'd trade a hundred of my father for my one son. I'd trade myself too though, so maybe that makes the admission less terrible.

I can make it more terrible if I really want to be honest. I used to hear Jim's anger and frustration and wish my father would go ahead and die and solve the problem. Only, of course, it wouldn't have, because the problem wasn't just made up of him—it took what Jim added to make it truly miserable. And what was that? I don't know if I can even see it accurately, let alone describe it. I guess the best I can do is call it an intolerance of ambivalence. Jim couldn't stand loving and hating the same person—the mixture was too rich, too volatile for him to bear. I think that's my fault. I think I needed Jim's love so much that I never gave him permission to hate me. I gave lip service to it—said he could disagree, stand up to me, argue—but I think, in his heart of hearts, he knew how much I counted on him to love me and think well of me. I depended on him for that because I couldn't always depend on myself for it.

I know a lot about ambivalence, about living with it. I guess, to be fair to myself, my parents never gave me permission to hate them either. I just learned that I sometimes did and that I could get by if I sequenced it. It's too hard to tolerate feeling the love and hate simultaneously. I did best if I just let it flip or flop according to whatever it was according to.

What should I have told Jim? Maybe that there's no virtue in suppressing hate or turning it back on yourself. Use it to fuel your escape. Let it burn itself out when you're so removed from its source that there's nothing combustible left. Whether you stay in one spot or physically remove yourself, put distance between you and its object and the hate will have nothing to live on except memories.

If you have to choose between yourself and others, choose yourself until you no longer perceive a choice. If you can only love one person, love yourself until your capacity is greater. And if you can't love anybody, at least be indifferent—it may save your life.

2–3–85    I'm at a conference. It's on a subject I need to know more about and it's fairly interesting. But I find my mind drifting off in the midst of things—thinking of Jim.

Yesterday, I walked around a mall during the lunch hour. I noticed lots of things, but most of all I noticed little boys. All ages, all sizes, all behaviors, all colorings—just little boys. And naturally, I thought of my own little boy.

I woke up yesterday morning, and as I lay there, unwilling to acknowledge to the cat that I was awake, I thought of a little boy thing that made me smile. We were flying, the first time for Jim and me and, as we circled the airport endlessly in a holding pattern, I got sick. I filled one bag and, since I was still sick, Jim (then Jimmy) stood up in his seat and said to the people behind us, "Excuse me, but my mother's sick. Would you give me a bag for her?" I was too helpless to ask and Hank was too confused or embarrassed, so my 6-year-old son rescued me.

The memory made me smile. And it wasn't followed by a self-rebuke—one of those rare times I allowed myself to remember how much I liked Jim without the corollary guilt.

To get back to other little boys—I kept looking at them and thinking how much I'd like to hug them or tell the parent with them to hug them, to say, "Don't be impatient with him. Don't criticize him. You have no idea how precious he is. I hope you're never confronted with that knowledge the way I was."

I thought of how angry I got with Jim a few years later when, during a plane change, he left behind all the things I had gotten to amuse him on a long trip. What was he then? Eight, I guess. I can't believe my stupidity—making a big deal out of it. It's one thing to drive yourself in a merciless quest for perfection. Why did I have to drive my dear little boy?

And yet, there's another side to the coin. I didn't drive Jim when it came to achievement, especially the scholastic kind. It was my niche and I knew the rigors I always went through, worrying about grades, worrying about what people thought of me intellectually, worrying about the fact that it's where my self-esteem originated. I believed that was wrong, too thin a thread, and I wanted Jim to know that he was good simply because he *was*, not because he gave proof of it in school.

I don't know how I messed up, but I figure I did. Time and again I heard he was "bright, but . . ." Teachers talked about motivation, always prefacing their pep talks with, "Jimmy's one of my favorite students" or "Jimmy's so likable." They always said (overtly or covertly), "Motivate him," and I'd feel frustrated (as I'm sure he did), finally asking, "How do I do that?" (I still don't know how anybody motivates anybody else.) I never hit on the right formula. I tried so much time for homework, money for good grades, no allowance for bad grades, questions, threats, pleas. I asked him if he wanted to see a psychologist, saying, "It's okay if you're upset with Dad and me," and I tried to listen when he did talk (which was rare to not at all).

Peggy tutored him. I just wasn't any good at it and she had prior experience with the crazy methods of one school he went to (I realize that's judgmental, but so be it. I believe most "education" is really just an attempt to subdue kids). My favorite Jim story of Peggy's is about the time they were working on something with which he was having difficulty. They went over and over the material. He finally got frustrated and said, "I hate this. I hate coming over here and covering this same stuff again and again when I just can't get it and I don't care."

She answered very patiently, "Well, I'm sorry, Jim, but we just have to keep at it until you *do* get it."

He grinned and shook his head, saying, "No, Aunt Peggy. This is where you're supposed to say, 'Well, I'm sorry, Jim, but if that's your attitude, I'll just have to ask you to leave and never come back.'"

I wish I'd tried other things—private schools, tutors, maybe even saying to him, "Don't give me any excuses. I know you're bright and I expect more from you than you're giving." (Nope, now that I think of it, I *did* say that.)

In any case, I want another chance. Not with another

child. Not with another person. Not to be a better psychiatrist or a better human being. I want another chance with Jim.

Oh, please let the Buddhists be right.

2–8–85    I got a letter from one of my friends, telling me that she had another friend whose son had committed suicide last year. She had just learned about it and said that she was at a loss to know what to say.

I answered, "I'll give you some advice, based on what has helped me—not as a psychiatrist, but as a bereaved mother.

First, don't remind her of her "blessings." Remind her of her strengths, her goodness and any positive things you may have observed in her relationship with her son. (She'll take care of remembering all the negative ones, believe me.)

Second, ask her how she's doing. Ask her what helps her. In the telling, those things will help her more.

Third, don't say, "I know how you feel," but if you've been bereaved, tell her what helped you. If both of you believe in prayer, say you'll pray for her.

Fourth, if you're comfortable doing it, tell her how you felt on learning the news. One of my friends said, "Oh, this is the most terrible thing I can imagine." It validated what I felt and focused on the event rather than my guilt as the "terrible thing."

Fifth, in case she doesn't know about them, tell her there are groups like Compassionate Friends and Survivors of Suicide that can offer support and information that may be invaluable to her. They can be contacted through the local Mental Health Association (they'll have the contact numbers).

Sixth, if it "fits" your feelings and friendship, invite

her for a visit. She doesn't have to take you up on it to benefit. To me invitations have been like a safety hatch—I know it's there if I ever need to escape.

Seventh, and probably most important, take your cue from her. If she wants to talk, listen. If she doesn't, leave it alone. The easiest way to know is to ask, "How are you doing?" If she answers, "Fine," and starts talking about something else, you know the door is closed for now.

2–10–85    Last weekend, as I drove to and from the conference, I thought about Emerson's phrase, "remove [my] bloated nothingness." I'd had such a hellacious week, felt so low, been tearing at myself—and I finally began to ask, "What makes you so important? Jim's life was separate from yours—why can't his decision be separate from you?"

When I got home, I called Peggy. I told her about these thoughts and she said, "I really don't think you had anything to do with it. I think Jim just didn't want to go on." That phrase echoed for hours in my mind—it is still echoing in fact.

The next morning Tom came in the bathroom just as I gave up on my hair. I expressed my frustration/disgust with it, then turned to leave the room. He put his hands on my shoulders and said, "There's nothing wrong with it. I'll be so glad when you get over this self-pity and get back to your normal self. You're really not entitled, you know—you have way too much going for you to feel this sorry for yourself." It made me so furious that I couldn't say a word. I just finished getting ready and left. Over the next day or two, I relived it and thought about what I was going to say when I had enough control to bring up the subject (meaning I figured I'd punch him in the mouth if I didn't calm down).

Then, I don't know, things just slid together and I realized they were both right. So was I. It's a personal loss but it wasn't a personal loss. The depth of my grief can only be known to me. I'm the one who was Jim's mother. But, Jim didn't take his life so I'd lose him. He did it for his own reasons.

How many ways must I say and hear these things before they become an article of faith? Sometimes that's so discouraging—the way I have to relearn everything over and over.

On the other hand, it's only been three months (minus six days). I wouldn't *let* myself re-equilibrate in that short a time—even if I could do so (which I seriously doubt). As the movie title implied, there are terms of endearment, bargains which love requires, and one of them is that those you love are invested with a part of you. Jim's death was my death as well as his own. And both require solemnity and thoughtfulness. The difficult thing is not to let that become grief for its own sake, the love of mourning which becomes display and self-pity. It's another term of endearment—respect for Jim and for myself. Those things I subsume under my guilt are taken from him. I diminish him in the process of becoming so all-important.

I got a letter from my niece Vona later in the week. I doubt she knew about the conversation Peggy and I had, but she's obviously on the same wavelength. I had sent her a copy of this journal and her letter was partially in response to that. She wrote:

I was surprised to see the part about my Dad in there. I appreciate the way you talk about going back to work. It's so hard to describe. When Papa died, I felt like if I didn't get up and go back to work when I did that I never would. It never fails to amaze me how people manage to say the exact right thing or exact wrong thing even though they are trying to help. It seems from the way you write you've had more of the first kind. . . . I feel fortunate that I had the upbringing I did. I'm one of the few people I know that doesn't hate their childhood and what they had to go through.

I want to say things to you as well as to Mom, Uncle David and even maybe to MaMaw—that would help you all feel less guilty. It's natural for you to feel but Jim was the only one that could have prevented what happened. I haven't studied suicide much—I know he had to be sending out signals—I also feel he may have sent them in a direction that he knew would do no good. Does that make sense? He knew Mom would know what was going on so he didn't go to her. He knew that Uncle David didn't know him well so he wouldn't realize how serious it was, and he probably felt that MaMaw and PaPaw wouldn't *listen*. I mean listen, not hear. He also knew that you would know and be able to stop him, thus he didn't seek help from you. I'm not sure when or how it reaches the point where a person decides nothing will stop him, but I feel Jim was at that point. I feel so sad that it happened and that it was the way it was. So alone, so determined, so positive. I interpreted the end (?) of his note the same way you did.

Well, I'm going to climb down off my soapbox and hush. Hang in there, keep plugging and all those other sayings.

Here's a memory that always makes me smile—the Christmas that Johnny and Jimmy decided to use PaPaw's head for a race track and got the car stuck in his hair.

Love, *Vona*

**2–15–85**     Peggy wrote me about the television film *Surviving,* which was about two families surviving the suicide deaths of their adolescent children. I commented on certain parts of it, then said, "It brought home the fact that there are some differences between teen suicide and adult suicide. I don't have that nailed down yet—it's more a sense of it than a well-thought-out rationale.

"Mostly I guess it has to do with the teen's greater melodrama and spite. I think there's a bigger percentage of 'I'll make them sorry for how they treated me' in the suicides of teens. For adults, suicide seems to hinge more on despair and a terrible self-criticism which becomes more than they can/are willing to tolerate. I may be wrong, but it seems different to me. I think it partially accounts for why teen suicides occur in clusters—the melodrama gets heightened. Adult suicides increase in the spring—a time of hope when one's lack of it becomes painfully (maybe unbearably) obvious."

2–25–85    Thoughts are coalescing now. Thoughts of wasteful, stupid, selfish—all of the things Jim wasn't by habit but was by his act.

There, in the center, is the self. The self Jim killed. The only self that concerned him at the time. It's so unfair—to him, to me, to all those who loved his other selves, who perhaps even loved that self.

How could my son *not* think of me? Confronted with the same choice, I thought of him. I try to answer—saying that, in that moment, in his emotional pain, he could only think of himself. But that's not good enough. We're grounded in the reality of others. We become ourselves in the mirrors of common existence, we are honed by the friction of our movements against and alongside others.

It's just that, there in that Slough of Despond, Jim made his declaration that no one, nothing, mattered more than his tightly clasped misery. All the world of possibilities was rejected. Not for him, the struggle to find meaning. Not for him, the everyday work of choosing good or bad, risk or safety, kindness or malice. Not for him, the responsibility of loving, of creating, of generating.

What he did will hurt me every day of my life. What he did inflicted on me the greatest suffering I can even imagine, much less have known. What he did has injured others I love and created a schism which may someday seal over, but will never heal for those of us who share in it. Things which were there before—secrets, things best ignored, things tolerated—are now too glaringly apparent. When I think of all the years I must pretend, I feel so angry. For I know it will *be* pretense. Pandora's box is open.

It was so wrong of Jim to upset the balance. If the game was intolerable, why not play something else? Maybe nobody can—switch games, I mean. But you can arm yourself, learn the rules, buy time, enter alliances, try out some other games so you'll see new patterns, etc., etc. Why did Jim's imagination have to be so limited? So many of my imaginings became reality. Why couldn't he take refuge in a fantasy long enough to save himself? Why couldn't he opt for something else like sticking out his thumb and seeing how far he could go and how fast he could get there? Why couldn't he leave a note saying, "Since you won't get off my back, I'm taking it to more congenial climes?"

Jim, how could you be so stupid? How could you waste your life that way? How could you hurt me this way? Is watching me your purgatory? I hope so.

**3–5–85**   I wrote Peggy and reminded her of an incident when Jim was about six or seven. I'd told him about Santa Claus and the Tooth Fairy, et al. He lost a tooth shortly after and asked what he should "do about it." I suggested with a wink that he put it under the pillow as usual and I'd pass the message along.

It completely slipped my mind and I was having coffee the next morning when he came in, holding up the tooth and saying, "Boy, that dumb old Tooth Fairy really blew it this time."

I contained my laughter and said, "Let's give her another chance. You go back to sleep and I'll give her a call."

After a few minutes, I tiptoed in. He was lying there, eyes tightly shut. I slipped the tooth out from under his pillow, substituting the money, then tiptoed out. Minutes later, he came out, triumphantly holding up the loot and saying, "Hey, she came through after all!"

I told my sister in the letter: "Sometimes I can't believe he's gone. That he let the reasons be reason enough. How can it be that he could see nothing else to do when the world is so full and there is so much which is beautiful?"

Richard Anderson said in *I Never Sang for My Father,* "Death ends a life, but it does not end a relationship—which struggles on in the survivor's mind toward some resolution which it may never find."

I had a sense of so much time for our resolution. I wanted to write of our relationship, to fictionalize what we did and looked like, to try and capture the essence of our love and conflict in words. Jim would read them and he would know my side of things—and gauge the accuracy of my perceptions about his side of things. I was bashful, thinking of it—but certain I would someday do it.

In a way my journal does it, but it's really only a glimpse—overshadowed by grief. How can it be that *I* am the survivor—struggling toward that resolution I may never find?

**3–8–85**   Jim, I have some things to say to you. Maybe you won't hear them and maybe you will, but I need to say them anyway—to you, from me.

I watched a World War II movie yesterday and I thought, as I've thought many times before, that if you had died in a war your death would have been easier for me to bear. Part of me questioned that at first and said, "No, the death of a child is the death of a child." Well, yes . . . and no.

If you had died in World War II, I could have blamed the Germans or the Japanese. If you had died in Korea, I could have blamed the Communists or North Koreans. If you had died in Vietnam, I could have blamed the Viet Cong or our own government. If you had died in a car wreck, I could have blamed Fate or the other driver. If you had died of an illness, I could have blamed the doctor or God.

Dying the way you did though, Jim, I can only blame you or us. I've gone through blaming us—and maybe I always will. But now the time has come when I can blame you.

Your life wasn't a waste, son—only the way you chose to end it. You gave me great joy. You taught me more about love than anyone else I've known because my love for you developed as we did.

I'm not the only one who loved you. I'm not the only one you hurt. And if you can hear me, and if you feel guilty, then so be it. If I can bear it, you can.

I feel disappointed in you. Sometimes I felt it before—probably less than you would believe. Now it's because you couldn't endure your suffering. Was it so much greater than anybody else's? Was the quantity so great or the quality so unique that you were justified in shifting it off onto us?

You weren't thinking of that. I know you weren't. What I want to know is, why not? What gave you the right to end the life I gave you and to take your future from me? Children don't belong to their parents? Oh yes, they do. We all belong to the people who love and create us. Only part of us belongs to ourselves.

Jim, I love you. I always did and I always will. When you were a little boy, you'd make me so angry sometimes. You've made me angry now. I think of the woman whose husband committed suicide. She paced around the house screaming and crying, "If you weren't dead already, I'd kill you for doing this to me!" Well, I wouldn't kill you, but I'd like to beat the tar out of you, my beautiful, beloved son.

**3–11–85** Sometimes I think of grief as a stone and all the helpful comments, all the loving moments with friends and family, all the good memories, all the meanings and purposes derived from it are water—dripping slowly—smoothing it over—then beginning to wear it away. Time is too short for the rock to wear away completely, but the erosion suffices.

**5–5–85** It's been a quiet time. Time I needed just to have my thoughts without examining or measuring them in words. Things have happened. A friend died, another had a son. How impersonal those personal events seemed—cycles of life and death which simply happen. Work continues, but the meaning is contained only in the doing.

I dreamed of Jim last night. I had gone to visit his grave, but it was unlike the real thing. All was above ground, like the graves in New Orleans. Somehow Jim was visible. I sat watching him until, slowly, he sat up and opened his eyes. I could see their unique green-brown color as he smiled. Then a transformation took place. He began to grow younger and younger, his mustache disappearing, his hair longer and then shorter. His face grew rounder and I recognized each age as he continued to smile. Finally he was a year old and he reached out his arms to me and I pulled him close and held him against my naked skin, his soft, smooth little body against me. I felt his silken hair and mouth against my breasts and then an orgiastic ecstasy as, once again, we became one.

I do contain his life. So much of these past few months has been a search through the last years of his life. So much has been an analysis of him, of myself, of the parts played by the other actors in his life. But there are so many memories, so many pictures of his face and it begins to register that I've been looking at a small portion of the total.

I finally reached a place where I wanted to know what he said to David the last day of his life. There were no real surprises. Most of the things that were eating him were current, having to do with my father and his frustrations. He said he wished I'd stayed married to Garland, given him a normal home life. That only told me he was think-ing with his emotions instead of his head. He recognized himself once that I couldn't live with his father and that, had we stayed together, it wouldn't have been a "normal home life." He had, in fact, teased me about it, saying, "I can't for the life of me imagine you married to him. You're so straight and he's such a wild man." Also, I had been through the guilt of "depriving" him of that (illu-sory) home since I divorced Garland twenty-four years before, so it wasn't a particularly raw nerve.

Jim also told David he wasn't sure about coming to stay with Tom and me—that he wasn't certain of his welcome. That also has its reality and its distortion. I had invited him and he knew that I had cleared it with Tom first. He also knew that, had he told us the alternative he was considering, both of us would have done anything to help. The reality is that he was twenty-five, that he had never lived with us, that he was sixteen and a half when we married, and that his relationship with Tom was a friendship rather than a stepfather–stepson relationship.

I focused for a while on the things David could have done, but then I recognized that he had done the best he could, the best Jim would let him. He said, "I think Jim picked me because he knew I would remember. He gave me pieces of the puzzle so I could fit them together later for you and the other people he loved." David acknowledged everyone's part, but concluded, "The only one with blood on his hands is Jim."

Amen.

# TWELVE

# Families and Forgiveness

HERE'S A BIT OF NEWS FOR YOU: Suicide occurs in healthy families. Depression is no respecter of age or circumstance, therefore its ultimate by-product can occur in any sort of family. We like to think it only occurs in sick ones, but we often base that notion on examination of a family flailing about in the agony of the aftermath. Sometimes it's a chicken-egg sort of argument. Which came first, the chaos or the suicide?

I can tell you that suicide doesn't do much for family cohesion, however. Some families pull together and deal with the crisis. Most don't. You might think of it as the opposite of Tolstoy's famous line: "All happy families resemble one another, but each unhappy family is unhappy in its own way." There is a deep family resemblance in most (unhappy) survivor families. They're alike in their guilt and blame and misdirected rage. They share a sense of abandonment and a fervent desire to have no more of it, even if it means pushing away the other survivors. They all too often keep their silence about the suicide, a conspiracy they enforce in myriad ways, often imposing years and years of silence on each other.

Treaters make a convenient target for these negative feelings.

That's the reason suicide is the most common reason for a malpractice suit against a mental health professional. I'm here to tell you that, although I may have some advantages when it comes to knowing what needs attention first, I (a) do not have a crystal ball, (b) am not omnipotent, and (c) am keenly aware that, although the person has often signaled suicidal thoughts, actually doing it is often impulsive and outside anyone's ability to intervene.

And of course, girlfriends are blamed, rock music is blamed, medication is blamed. Characteristically, parents blame each other—at least part of the time. Every old wound is opened, every communication problem is exaggerated. It is not surprising that people sometimes divorce or split apart in some other way. What is surprising is that it doesn't happen in every case.

As I mentioned, secrecy often rules, and survivors have suffered in silence for decades, unable to acknowledge the suicide, let alone their feelings about it. Imagine, if you will, the impact this has on those tenuous lines of communication we have with others. If we never talk about the most painful and deeply felt event of our lives with our father, mother, brother, sister, mate, or child, how are we to be "real" to them? They, like every stranger, will only see our surface, so that achieving true intimacy with them becomes impossible.

Survivors may choose to make emotional cutoffs which are either total or partial. That is, they may block out everyone in their family or simply end their involvement with the individuals they consider the most problematic. I think the first is potentially fatal, but the second may be highly adaptive at the time, especially if the particular relationship has always been a troubled one. It takes energy to work out longstanding problems, and such energy may not only be in short supply (especially the first few years) but may be better spent on something the survivor gives higher priority, like healing him or herself, fostering the next generation, helping other survivors.

The decision to cut off a portion of the family can always be reversed later, but we would do well to remember that it takes two to have a dialogue. Just because one party to a dispute changes or grows, it doesn't mean the other party has covered an equal amount of ground. And nobody can make you crazier faster than your family—ambivalence again. If a survivor decides to reverse a cutoff decision, he or she would be well advised to move at what a friend of mine calls "glacial speed." Millimeter forward (as opposed to "inch forward") and be prepared to be very, very patient with those not-so-loved-ones.

Someone once said that the suicide puts his skeleton in other people's closets. I think that's true. That skeleton is especially burdensome if it's added to skeletons that were already there. When that's the case and there are pre-existing abusive or painful elements in a relationship, no one has the right to come along and enjoin forgiveness. I cannot tell you how much damage I've seen people do by prescribing forgiveness for others. Whatever the offense, be it incest, assault, emotional abuse, or suicide, it's up to the survivors, whether or not they feel like forgiving the affront. They know the virtues of forgiveness; they also know whether or not they're ready to do it.

If someone says to me, for instance, that I need to forgive my father for his contributions to Jim's suicide, I am immediately angry, then guilty. I am angry because they are being presumptuous. If they knew all the facts, they might not be so quick to judge my hard feelings. If they were in my shoes, they might, in fact, even be vengeful. And if they had seen my restraint, shown because not to show it would have meant extending the damage Jim's suicide did to him and the rest of my family, they might even marvel at the deep kindness that restraint represented.

On the other hand, I feel guilt when I'm told to forgive my father because I know I'm not up to the task. I'd like to be able to do it since I've been steeped in a tradition that regards a forgiving nature as a virtuous one. Most Americans share that view— though they don't, perhaps, share that virtue. That's why prescribing it to any survivor is such a trap. Victimization from any cause damages self-esteem. If you heap on top of that an injunction to do something the survivor can't do, you guarantee another loss of self-esteem.

To say the least, this is not helpful.

I have no idea how much my father blames himself. When Jim died, I heard nothing in my father's words to suggest that he accepted any blame, but I imagine that somewhere in his conscience, he knows his portion. The only thing my mother said about it to me was in a letter. She wrote, "We loved him so, but somehow we failed him. That's what breaks our hearts. . . ."

I wanted to help her, partially because she's my mother and partially because it's my nature to help people whatever my relationship to them. I wrote back.

Yes, I suppose we did fail Jim. I've spent months torturing myself with all the ways *I* did. But Jim also failed us and himself. He didn't have to choose the option he did. He didn't have to embrace his misery. We all have to deal with our self-destructive urges if we're going to live a reasonably sane life. Jim didn't deal with it—he took it to its limit—and he's to blame for that. It was *his* choice. It never would have been ours.

Sometimes I'm angry at the two of you. Sometimes I'm angry at his father and stepfather. Most of the time I'm angry at myself. Now I'm beginning to be most angry at Jim. It's anger tinged with regret. I don't want to feel it. I'd give anything if Jim were there instead of that anger, but I know he's gone and that's what I'm stuck with. That's what makes me angriest of all—that I'm stuck with something that affects me so profoundly and yet I had no say-so in the matter. By the time I knew Jim was dying, he was dead.

If whatever we did or failed to do was unbearable to Jim, he should have told us. You can't correct something you don't know about or read someone else's mind. I'd have much preferred being told to go to hell rather than trying to interpret what Jim was saying to me with his act. I know I'm a tougher judge of myself than he would have been, therefore I figure I'd have been less tortured by his indictments than I am by my own.

# THIRTEEN

# Ranging Far and Wide

CAN I SAY THAT I'm an educated person? I think it's just a statement of fact, given that I went to college five and a half years, medical school four years, and did a residency that included a lot of classroom time for four years.

That doesn't mean that I remember more than a portion of what I've learned. It just means I know where to look. That's the real benefit of a higher education. You learn where and when to look.

This gives me an advantage. But an even greater one is what someone called a "tolerance for ambiguity." Some people have it, some people don't. I have it in spades.

Ambiguity, if you looked it up, means that which is uncertain or vague and has two or more possible meanings. I might say that the fact that I'm a psychiatrist accounts for my awareness that few things are absolute, but I suspect the truth is that I became a psychiatrist because I already thought that. You have to think that or you would never be able to tolerate the messiness of people's lives, the way they feel love at one second and hate at the next. Hence, without it, you would never go into this field.

Tolerating ambiguity means taking things the way you find them. You don't assume they'll stay that way or that they were always that way. That's just the way they are at the time you're examining them. There's little point in trying to make everything appear consistent—something *has* to be left out in order to pull that off. The best we can do is come up with an average, meaning that the situation or person is a certain way more times than it or he is not.

Both of those things—my education and tolerance for ambiguity—mean that, when I lost my son to suicide, I knew where to look and I knew how to accept what I found on its own terms.

Tom used to joke that I was the only person he knew who didn't just say she liked poetry but actually read it. And, not long ago, I mentioned something I'd read that day by Wordsworth, only to have my dinner companion grin and say, "You think that's *normal?* Reading Wordsworth?"

Poetry helped me when Jim died. I've already mentioned those that meant the most to me, but they might not be the ones that would stir your heart. I think we find what we need. If you were suffering and you picked up a book of poetry, you might start leafing through it and something would guide you to the one you need to read. I'd apologize for sounding mystical about that, but I *am* mystical about that.

I collected things in my journal. They look like a hodge-podge, but they are exactly the blend of things I needed. There's humor by Mark Twain, some thoughts and a selection of poetry from a friend, an assortment of newspaper columns Walt Menninger sent me about Compassionate Friends, translations of Buddhist scriptures, excerpts from Karl Menninger's *Love Against Hate,* correspondence from friends with my answers recorded, dreams I had and which I sometimes interpreted and sometimes didn't, thoughts sparked by reading C. S. Lewis's account of his wife's death and his dawning awareness that he could only sense her presence when he suspended his grieving.

One of the letters I recorded was from Karl Menninger. He was one of the "friends" I sent my letter and poem to, and I mentioned in a postscript that his book had helped me. He wrote,

I am glad that you wrote me about it. It gave me great comfort to know that I had helped you in this crisis. Your strong spirit of humanity shows in the way you reacted to it. Your poem was so eloquent, one of the most moving I have ever read.

After a while, write me again. Tell me what you are doing. You have to do something, you know. You *will* do something, little things. You will do greater things than you think.

I respect the dignity of your suffering, expressed by your letter, and I won't keep talking. But I am still here. And I will be thinking of you. Come if you should want to.

I felt very blessed by that letter, as I always felt blessed by knowing "Dr. Karl."

But to get back to the writings of C. S. Lewis, I decided to try his method of suspending grief and letting in the presence of the "lost" one. It worked. It was really prosaic as it turned out. I couldn't get my hair to suit me another morning and said, "Oh, Jim. What am I going to do?" And it felt as though he put his arm over my shoulder as he said, a laugh in his voice, "Hair isn't everything, Mom." I quipped, "Easy for you to say," and turned to see Tom, a puzzled expression on his face. I said, "I'm talking to Jim." He said, "Right," and went back to his reading.

David had several experiences which were both inexplicable and, in one instance, frightening. Once, he went to Jim's grave to clear out some weeds and plant a little holly bush. When he and his wife, Lynda, got back in his car, it was filled with the scent of flowers, despite the fact there were none around. He said Jim was saying thanks and Lynda agreed. Another time, he was bathing and had the sense Jim had walked in the room and sat down, wanting desperately to communicate with him. David told me it felt so eerie that he was unnerved and had said, "Jim, I understand that you want to communicate something to me, but this is scaring the hell out of me." He said Jim immediately left the room and never came back—and he apologized to me, saying, "I'm sure you'd like to know what he was trying to get across, but I just couldn't handle it." I told him it was okay and it was.

Right after he told me, I wrote in my journal:

> I find my brother's experience comforting. Though I can postulate "reasons" for it, I'm content not to do so. It's a door that I want left open. What if there is another reality than the one I know? What if there are distances within death? Perhaps our loved ones can be close enough to touch the invisible barrier and set up a resonance that reaches one of us. Maybe if I suspended my doubt and guilt, I could feel it too. Or maybe I did when I had those dreams in which Jim reassured me he was all right. Maybe time and death are only waking illusions, and the unconscious sees things as they truly are; past, present, and future intermingled, the dead and the living co-existing.

I had the very strong sense that Jim visited me in my dreams a few times. Several years later a fellow psychiatrist sent me a book called *On Dreams and Death* by Marie-Louise von Franz. It was a fascinating account of the dreams preceding death and dreams that informed the person a death had taken place, often half a world away. The author, a Jungian analyst, interpreted these dreams in terms of Jung's theories that a timeless (and therefore eternal) universe co-exists with our time and body-bound universe—and that those within each communicate sometimes in dreams. It was especially interesting to me in light of the journal entry I quoted above, since I hadn't read Jung at the time I wrote that. I find his way of stating it both comforting and, in some ways, congruent with my experience. You may say that I need to see it that way, since each of Jim's "visitations" was reassuring and helpful. I won't argue with you, nor will I try to convince you of the "reality" of these things. I neither know nor care how real they are. I know they helped.

Finally, there was an experience that is even more inexplicable than those. I wrote about it in a column entitled "The Lens," published in December of 1990. I'd rather reproduce it than describe it because it's one of those stories that deserves a full telling. To wit:

———

Not long ago, I said something about "witnessing" in a letter to a Jewish pen-pal. He wrote back that he didn't know what it meant. It gave me pause, as I once again realized how we take it for granted that everyone grew up with the same concepts we did.

My folks weren't churchgoers when I was a kid, but they had been steeped in church tradition and my father considered himself "back-slid." I went to Sunday school occasionally and Vacation Bible School when I was eight or nine. The only two things I recall from that experience were making an elephant-shaped pincushion for my mother and memorizing the 23rd Psalm. I was a memorizing fool and memorized *The Night Before Christmas* in the fourth grade just for grins. I remember astounding my teacher when I told her I'd done it. She asked me to recite the poem for the class and I did. Gosh, what a little nerd. . . .

Pardon the pun, but the pincushion sticks in my memory because the "stuffing" was my hair. The oils in said-same are supposed to make the pins slide in and out more easily. (Cut me some slack here, okay?) There was something so gratifying about that—giving my mother a gift made from a part of myself. I had times when I whispered that I hated her, but mostly I loved her desperately and knew it full well. A potent force, my mother—intelligent and willful and with a pride that was often overweening. I look like her and, after years of struggle, I accept that in many, many ways I am not only like her, but proud of it. I'll come back to her (as I invariably do) in a minute.

I wrote my Jewish friend the following:

I suppose "witnessing" (to me anyway) means to declare one's own painful or revelatory experiences to others in an effort to illuminate the path for someone else. It's a tenet of Christianity—which is, after all, based on the idea of a sacrifice (Jesus' death) in order to wash away our sins. In the Catholic faith, confession is done privately and expiation given—all of it remaining within a dyadic relationship with the priest representing God. For a Protestant (especially in the more fundamentalist versions), confession is done publicly for the betterment of the community of listeners—to bring the spirit of God into their midst. "We are all sinners here. I declare my sins today as a token for the sins of each." Don't know if that makes any sense to you, but that's the idea.

He said my explanation made sense, even if the basic premise didn't. That made me smile since I've often had the same thought. I think the concept metamorphosed in me, retaining the best remnants of itself, but becoming more humanistic or pantheistic as I went through a life characterized by more than average turbulence (I acknowledge that a generous portion of that was of my own making).

The fact is that all suffer, but some folks are the acknowledged champs. I think of two women a psychiatrist friend of mine interviewed on videotape. One had lost her two children in a car-train accident and the other had suffered violent sexual abuse by her father. Listening to them was like watching Phoenix rise from the ashes. I think I'd get consensual validation for saying that I'm one too (at least a lightweight champ), having lost my only child to suicide. People always say, "How terrible!" They're right. But, it doesn't take *that* event to get something out of this quote from Robert Frost (in which God is trying to explain to Job why he visited such suffering on him):

> Society can never think things out:
> It has to see them acted out by actors,
> Devoted actors at a sacrifice—
> The ablest actors I can lay my hands on.

What sustains us if not our ideas? I found the idea of being a devoted, able actor a compelling one and one which gave meaning to my suffering. Not that it compensated me—nothing can compensate me—but it gave me some sense of purpose. I sort of raised my bloodied head, looked about me and said, "Okay, Sue. If you can't nurture your son, maybe you can nurture the abstractions you believe in. Maybe the point for you is to live that part of the 23rd Psalm that says, "Surely goodness and mercy shall follow me all the days of my life."

In the immediate stages of my grief, I unconsciously paraphrased another verse from the Bible and found myself whispering, "I shall lift up mine eyes to the commonplace, whence comes my help." And that was exactly what my heart meant. Not the hills, not the divine, but the everyday forces of good and love and daily effort. Kindness. Thoughtfulness. Respect. Those human things, those myriad small acts and words which collectively make the world worth inhabiting and without which I literally could/would not go on living.

That's what I value. That's what I try to live. I once had a patient tearfully say, "Thank you for remembering me." She meant that with her former therapist, she was forgotten in the intervals between appointments. Each time, the therapist's questions revealed that basic information had slipped her mind—to say nothing of the patient's pain and confusion. No goodness and mercy there.

In the larger world—in contacts with colleagues and the nurses on the unit and the paper boy—in all those random intersections of my life with other lives, I *try*. I don't always succeed. I get distracted and preoccupied with myself. But I try. Sometimes, after yoga, I meditate and silently say, "I am filled with light. I will let that light shine through me and illuminate the lives of others. It does not come from me. It does not stay with me. It only passes through me." I am, in effect, a lens. That's what witnessing is about—being as good a lens as one can.

There's a logic in that metaphor, isn't there? Think about how most lenses are made. The glass is produced by fusing silicates (sand, for instance) with soda or potash, lime, and sometimes various metallic oxides. Nothing fancy. Then, it's heated to tremendous temperatures and, once in the correct shape, it's cooled and polished. Sounds like a human to me. What do you think?

I'm not, despite moments when I refract very well, especially brilliant. But I know that the goal is transparency, and that is (in those moments I can get myself out of the way) my gift. It's so difficult, given my acculturation—which is to say, my ego. Everything bids me to credit myself and to accept the credit of others. In our society, all good things are "achievements" and the product of our efforts.

It isn't true.

The Rune saying is true: "What is yours will come to you."

I didn't know I believed that so strongly until something came to me, something which would not have come had I not believed in that principle. In my capacity as a lens, I'll tell you about it. But don't misunderstand me: I do not regard this as a revelation in the religious sense. Such things are, I think, a platform for those who are promulgating beliefs they feel are universal. What came to me and what is mine is a personal illumination—an enrichment of *my* experience rather than a credo of any spiritual community. I don't share it with you to persuade you to anything. I share it because I sense it's right to do so. I've always thought I should find a way to tell others, but until now, I couldn't see that way. I guess I hadn't been polished enough.

For months after my son died, every dream I had of him was filled with the knowledge of his death. Whatever age, whatever context, I viewed him with the aching awareness that he was dead, often awakening with a chest-crushing pain, sometimes crying out, sometimes simply moaning.

One morning, I awakened like that, my whole body so rigid with agony that I couldn't move, couldn't even spare the energy it took to open my eyes. It was so absorbing, that pain, so consuming that there was no *me* left in it. And, then, seemingly out of nowhere, I thought, "Saint Sebastian." Just that. Something eased and my mind said the name again. Another easing. I had no idea where it came from, what it meant, who he was. All I knew was that if I said his name over and over I was relieved. So, I did—until, eventually, I fell into a dreamless sleep and woke up, refreshed.

Oddly enough, I didn't think about it, didn't puzzle over it, didn't concern myself with it. I went about my business, did my work, ate my meals, talked with my family and friends. Then, I dreamed about Jim and it was just a Jim-dream, just a little-devil dream as he teased me—a baby, a boy, a young man. He liked to tease me and started early. He could always make me laugh, my Jimbo, Jimmy, Jim. In the dreams, he made me laugh again and my broken heart was eased, knowing he was restored, at least in my sleep. Thank you, I said. Far be it from me to look a gift horse in the mouth, I said. I'm grateful for this much, I said.

I meant it from the bottom of my Humpty Dumpty heart. I still do.

Then, one day I asked a Catholic friend if she knew how Saint Sebastian had achieved sainthood. She didn't She told me to ask so-and-so. I asked them. They didn't know either. I let it drop. Weeks, maybe a month or two, went by—then, driving past the library one day, I wheeled in and parked, thinking, "Oh, what the heck, I'm tired of this nagging me. I'll just run in and look it up."

I didn't find him in the first book. There was something vague in the second. I don't remember much about it—early Christian martyr. Then, as I opened the third, I found a small black and white picture of a painting alongside a few paragraphs. And it was as though something immense slammed into me. I plunked down cross-legged on the floor, trying to keep my heart in my chest by pressing it with my hand—while tears sprung to my eyes. In the picture, Sebastian is tied to a tree, his body riddled with arrows. And, I read that he was sentenced to death for his beliefs, ostensibly "executed" in this way and left to hang from the tree as an example. Another Christian, a woman, cared for him and he recovered from his wounds, once again witnessing his faith until he was ultimately killed.

As I looked at him, I silently cried out, "Yes! That's

how I feel! Riddled with arrows, left for dead!" It was always incredible to me that no one seemed to see my arrows. They might know I'd been shot, but they couldn't see the arrows. To me, it felt like they must be sticking out every which way. I'd try to describe them, but I realize now that I did it in a academic way, telling the person, "I'm riddled with arrows, you know." They'd say politely, "Oh, dear. Is there anything I can do?" And I'd answer, "No, thank you. I've gotten accustomed to them."

I don't know why I didn't just scream. Just scream and scream and scream until they were compelled to see the arrows and do something about them. Surely each friend would have pulled one out and put on some salve. I had enough friends to do the job.

No, that isn't true. I do know why. I told you I'd come back to my mother again. *She* taught me not to scream. I still don't do it well. The few times I've had surgery, I apologized to everyone around me for groaning. I'd throw up and moan, "I'm sorry. I'm sorry." It's driven my husband crazy.

It's not a good way to be. It shuts you inside yourself and convinces everybody dear to you that you don't need them. Gets you in lots of trouble—not knowing how to scream. I can, of course, point that tendency out to others better than I can change it in myself. I had a patient tell me once that she shouldn't *have* to do it, that if she were truly loved, her distress would be heard. I shook my head, smiled a little, and said, "Hey, even a well-loved baby has to yell sometimes."

Oh, if only insight truly altered us.

But, to get back to St. Sebastian—the inability to scream was only a narrow band of the light streaming into me as I looked at his picture. Eventually, I was able to see the full spectrum. And what I saw was the blessed fact that, however grievous my wounds, I could live with them, I could witness again, I could be a miracle of tenacity, a model of how to just plain old hang on for dear life. Because life *is* dear. Whatever else it is, whatever arrows pierce me, my life is dear. What is mine comes to me. Including life itself.

My son couldn't see that. Or seeing it, he closed his eyes and called it a hallucination which had no bearing on his painful reality. In effect, he closed the shutter and the light couldn't enter.

Other people only open part way, thinking the light's too strong or too weak. If too strong, they believe they must shield themselves from it. If too weak, they try to husband what they have.

What can I witness to them?

Maybe that life isn't a camera, but a telescope—a marvelous array of lenses. We have to look for every glimmer, every pinpoint of light in the vastness and magnify it again and again and again in our effort to truly perceive it. How can we, looking out at a space teeming with stars, call it a Void? And how can we, gazing around us, not be dazzled by the blazing aspirations of humanity?

I can only generate a faint and flickering light. But turn me just so and my surface, perfectly abraded in those moments when I've given up my ego and surrendered to life's friction, collects the radiant energy of universal goodness and mercy and casts forth a pure, unassailable beacon which witnesses that we are all children of the light.

The Lord is our shepherd; we shall not want.

He maketh us to lie down in green pastures; he leadeth us beside the still waters.

He restoreth our souls.

# FOURTEEN

# Responsibility

ONE OF THE CONCEPTS I've always appreciated is that you have to put your money where your mouth is. I have no patience with people who say one thing and do another. I know that's not unique to the part of the country where I grew up, but sometimes I've thought it derived from the Code of the West. In less civilized places, a person's word had to be his bond and that idea became part of the ambiance—we who follow a generation or two later absorb it as we walk the same land.

So I've felt very strongly that I had to do certain things and behave a certain way, based on the things I learned from surviving Jim's suicide.

For one, so much of what rankles in suicide is the way the suicide shirks his responsibility to say goodbye. Sounds strange, doesn't it? It is nonetheless true. The person always exits precipitously and the survivors never have time to brace themselves the way they do when someone is dying of an illness. Of course, suicide isn't the only form of sudden death. It's just the only one where the dead person chose it. If you think a wife is angry at her heart-attack-victim husband for abandoning her, you should get a load of what she feels when he shoots himself in the head. *Big* difference.

Suicide feels like a preemptive strike. One resents not having a chance to negotiate. That's what goodbye really is: a chance to negotiate, to say, "It's like this with me, what's it like with you? I need to go now. Is there anything we need to settle before I leave?"

I don't think Americans typically do that well. I didn't before I understood it better. As a military wife, I used to beg the question, saying I'd probably see my friends somewhere else, given the surprisingly insular nature of the Army. People you've been stationed with at one place *do* have a way of showing up at the next one. Still, such things are uncertain and there were plenty of people I never saw again. I wish I'd done a better job of saying goodbye to them.

After Jim died, I began to take saying goodbye very seriously. And so, when I decided I wanted to move away from the clinic where I had worked for three years, I gave nine months' notice and then hung in there with my friends and patients, allowing them to say what they needed to and saying what I needed to say.

I wrote what is still my favorite column on that subject. It ends this way:

I think of the most painful termination of all—the death of someone we love. Nothing brings home more clearly the concepts that "though much is taken, much abides," and that we are all a part of all that we have met. I've sometimes heard, and sometimes said, "But, I didn't get to say goodbye!" When I'm thinking, I ask, "Who does?" because I recognize that saying goodbye is not a moment—it's a process. It's an echo down canyon walls and into the depths of caves, magically vibrating the air for years and coming back to us in waves, often when we least expect it.

We lose and we keep. We let go and we hold on. And, from time to time, we examine what we're holding. Sometimes, it's trash. Sometimes, it's treasure.

I hold some jewels. A sidelong glance, an "I love you, too," the memory of laughter, a tingling recollection of beloved flesh in my fingers. I feel enormous loss. And I feel enormous gratitude. For having had love. For having had my capacity enlarged, however painful the expansion may have been.

None of us gives our permission for life to happen to us. Nobody's going to tell us *why*. But, I have a feeling T. S. Eliot was right when he said:

> We shall not cease from exploration
> And the end of all our exploring
> Will be to arrive where we started
> And know the place for the first time.

I think that, the more we leave, the more we remain with ourselves. And, in a curious way, the more we leave, the closer we come to those we have left and those who have left us. And when we come to rest in that first and final place, I think we will finally perceive the fact that, during all our travels, the electrons of those we have loved were orbiting gently through our hearts.

In addition to learning the importance of saying goodbye properly, I often wished psychiatrists were better trained in dealing with survivors. I know they aren't well trained because I knew I wasn't, despite the fact that I had done my residency at what is arguably the best training institution in this country. I had done okay with the survivors I'd seen before Jim's death, but my work was based on general rather than specific information and, though I apologize for the conceit, on my intuitive grasp of the things which kill the soul.

Because I learned which things helped me as a survivor and studied the process in me even as it happened, I felt it was incumbent upon me to teach my profession those hard-won lessons. For that reason, I wrote a paper on surviving and read it at the Menninger Alumni Celebration in 1986. They published it in their bulletin the next year. I also presented that same paper at the American Association of Suicidology, an organization I joined in 1986 because of my belief that only through sharing my feelings and information could I withstand the things I had to withstand.

It's like a little story in Kushner's *When Bad Things Happen to Good People.* In it, a woman loses her only son and is overwhelmed by her grief. She goes to a holy man and asks him to bring her son back to life. He tells her to fetch a mustard seed from a home which has never known sorrow; with that they will drive the sorrow from her life. Naturally, she can't find such a home, but she's stirred by each family's story of tragedy and stays to comfort those she meets. Ultimately, of course, she heals her own sorrow by ministering to others.

In a sense, I minister to other psychiatrists through my column, writing about the emotional side of being a psychiatrist, sharing my viewpoint and experiences, and in the process, making it okay to be human. The letters and feedback I've received say they wanted somebody to do that.

I wrote an article to help doctors work more effectively and compassionately with bereaved parents, which was published in a magazine that goes to all residents, interns, and medical school faculty in the United States. It was reprinted in another that reaches all the members of the Texas Medical Association.

Somewhere along the way, I realized that I now identify myself as a bereaved parent first, a psychiatrist second. If you met me and felt compelled to understand me, you'd do a better job of it by knowing the former rather than the latter. That's interesting, since most people have a lot of preconceived notions about psychiatrists and very few about bereaved parents other than their predictable pain. What the general public seldom thinks about is the multiplicity of things people do with that pain.

The pain has both softened and toughened me. I am, I think, gentler with those who need my compassion. But I am far more likely to challenge the person who simply feels sorry for him or herself. I see such persons going down the same dead-end street Jim traveled; if their brakes are faulty, I'll slam on mine to get their attention. I think I'm infinitely more effective with suicidal patients than I used to be. I always knew how to do the crisis intervention part, meaning breaking things down into pieces small enough so that the patient could do something about them and get un-overwhelmed. What Jim's death enabled me to do is to get out of the position of ultimate responsibility.

I said before that I hear even very experienced therapists talk about "keeping patients alive." We *don't* keep patients alive. We ally ourselves with what is healthy and strong and wants to live. We try to punch that up. However, if the urge to die is stronger, there is absolutely no way we can keep them alive. Nobody can do that for anybody; it's a dangerous illusion to think that we can. It's dangerous because, if the scales tip too far in favor of dying, we will assume that's our fault; the subsequent guilt will damage us and render us less effective with others who would take our help.

Bear in mind that I am not talking about the patient who is psychotic, so out of touch with reality that he can't make *any* decision, let alone the one to live or die. It is incumbent upon the members of my profession that we take whatever measures we must to protect those people from themselves. I have committed such people to the hospital, told them I was going to keep them safe whether they cursed me or blessed me for that, said that I would tie them up and sit on them if I had to. That is a qualitatively different situation from the depressed person considering suicide. Argue if you want to that depression is also a form of mental illness. I know that. I also know that the vast majority of depressed people are not psychotic and are therefore not out of touch with reality.

I see all kinds of people who threaten suicide as an expression of their unhappiness or rage. My job is to help them do something about that unhappiness and rage, to channel it, if you will, into effective action.

I recently saw a young woman who keeps her therapist on the brink of panic with her "hints" about suicide and statements that life isn't worth living, that she'd be better off dead, etc. She said of her therapist, "She can't understand why I want to die."

I know the patient well, having been her doctor during a

hospital stay, and I responded, "I understand it perfectly. You haven't even *started* to solve your problems."

Surprised, she asked me what I meant and I went on to confront her about her lack of effective action on any of a host of things we'd talked about when she was in the hospital. She was letting everything slide, waiting for everybody around her to straighten up and fly right, and she was taking *no* responsibility for herself. I said, "The only person who can get you unstuck is *you*, and you're going to be suicidal as long as you're stuck."

It was not a gentle approach and it's yet to be seen whether or not it was an effective one. I just know that the sympathetic approach of her regular therapist is totally ineffective, since the therapist is the one doing all the work and taking all the responsibility.

That is Jim's legacy to my professional life, just as it can be his legacy to you if you're a suicide survivor. Having worked through the fact that I was not responsible for my son's killing himself makes me not responsible for anyone killing himself. Knowing that in my bones gives me relative immunity from the anxiety most therapists feel on that issue.

# FIFTEEN

# When You're Falling, Dive

---

SOMETIMES I TELL MY PATIENTS that life is not a linear progression—we don't travel one way along a nice neat line from 0 to 92 (or whatever). Life is more spherical (or elliptical?). We have a core; over that we form layer after layer. Sometimes the core radiates out its messages, sometimes a layer isn't smoothly formed, but we contain the totality of our existence—all thoughts, all feelings, all memories. All that we have met is a part of us. It's why an eighty year old sometimes looks out at the world in childlike wonder. It's why adults can and need to play. And it's why we're sometimes childish and spiteful, sometimes grandiose and self-deluded about our own omnipotence. It's why, if you don't settle an earlier issue, it'll come back to haunt you. Like my attempt to gain independence by marrying at fifteen—it was a short-cut, and like all developmental short-cuts, it left the job largely undone, so that I had to grapple with independence again and again—long past the point when it should have been settled. I think Jim struggled with the same issue, but he postponed instead of jumping the gun—until his postponement became too painful and he could only separate by dying.

Most of us live our life in fits and starts. We go along and play it safe for years at a time. We let problems go underground until they become a teeming goo that bubbles up and engulfs us. Strangely enough (when you think about it), we tend to live as though our life is a rehearsal for the real thing. We're always "going to do something" next month, next year, next decade.

In my family, our parents always assured us they were only waiting for us to grow up so they could divorce. Well, I was the last one to leave home—in January of 1958—and they're still together.

All this is by way of saying, "Get a grip!" It's all well and good to ponder your situation and have dazzling insights into how you got the way you are. It's quite another to change, and that's usually what we need desperately to do.

I just wrote a speech I'm going to give at a survivors (of suicide) conference, and I'd like to share it with you here. It's titled, "When You're Falling, Dive."

———

Last year I gave a speech on surviving suicide at the American Association of Suicidology, then several months later I delivered the same paper in San Francisco and Chicago. In it, I mentioned that, despite my son's suicide six and a half years ago (indeed, perhaps because it forced me to), I believe in the benignancy of the universe. That is, I believe there is something good and sustaining in an overall sense, even if, at individual moments, we are devastated by malign events. A woman came up to me after one of these speeches and asked how I could reconcile something as terrible as suicide with my belief in a benign universe. I answered (inadequately, I imagine) that I thought one just had to assume it, to take a "leap of faith" and tell oneself that immediate experience was only a thread in the total weave. The tapestry is, I think, quite beautiful. It isn't diminished by those individual threads which desolate us.

I thought later of a poem I cited once in my column. It's by John Masefield and says:

I have seen flowers come in stony places
And kind things done by men with ugly faces,
And the gold cup won by the worst horse at the races,
So I trust, too.

If you will note, Masefield doesn't change the stony places to fertile ones; he doesn't say those faces are pretty after all; the worst horse is still the worst to start with. He's saying, consider that there may be more here than meets the eye. *That's* how I'm able to believe in the benignancy of the universe—knowing that the apparent is not the only possible reality.

I, like you, am insulted by someone else's effort to depreciate my pain and devalue my experience by saying that everything happens for the best, that although I've lost a son, I'm a better person for it. That may, in some sense, be true. It just isn't anybody else's call. For that reason, I am not setting out to convince you that you should believe what I do. Believe it if it suits you. Believe something else if that something else serves you better.

My view simply works for me. Since my son died, I have read and thought and written some strange things. He forced me to think about that which is unseen and intangible, yet perhaps no less real than his flesh and green-brown eyes were. His death caused me to smile knowingly when I read these words by Ursula LeGuin:

Which is farther from us, farther out of reach, more si-lent—the dead, or the unborn? Those whose bones lie under the thistles and the dirt and the tombstones of the Past, or those who slip weightless among molecules, dwelling where a century passes in a day, among the fair folk, under the great, bell-curved Hill of Possibility?*

I don't know where Jim is and, at times, I believe my sense of where I am is only illusion, even though it is consensually validated. He is dead. I am alive. End of story.

Well, perhaps. But you should try reading Jung. If you can get past some of the convolutions of his language, you will find that he talks rather convincingly of co-existent universes and of a psyche which so intensifies at death that it transcends the velocity of light and leaves the body, crossing into the timeless and therefore eternal realm. He goes even further, suggesting that in dreams our psyches sometimes cross the barriers between these differing states, communicating and perceiving things otherwise unknown and unknowable. We're aware dreams are often memories and restore the past to us, but Jung is saying that they may also contain the future (and when we recall them, those dream residues are called precognitions) or an altered present—altered in the sense of being populated by people who, in our waking life, are gone.

Many of us have had dreams in which the dead are with us so vividly that we awaken feeling as though they've just stepped from the room. Those dreams in which I had the strongest sense of my son, Jim's, presence were very comforting to me. Those which were merely *about* him had the opposite effect, inducing an agony of guilt. Those sensations or convictions or whatever you would call them are, perhaps, not okay to talk about if one

*Ursula LeGuin, *Always Coming Home* (New York: Bantam Books, 1986).

cares about his or her "scientific credibility," but I remain impressed by them and they have educated me to the existence of what someone called "rationally impenetrable mysteries." It is not a tremendous leap from those mysteries to some notion of a cosmic consciousness. And given the profoundly comforting nature of those mysterious dreams which come from who knows where and touch me in who knows what way, I intuit that the cosmic consciousness they manifest is strengthening, loving, and benign.

One of my favorite Rilke poems conveys the idea perfectly:

> Be—and yet know the great void where all things begin,
> the infinite source of your own most intense vibration

Is that not a description of something truly divine? Not a figurehead or a set of rules, but a source with which we resonate in an unparalleled harmony when we give ourselves over to it, when we follow Rilke's injunction to *be* and yet *know*. To be and yet know is the essence of our individual consciousness and it aligns us with the cosmic consciousness.

I will confess to you—I am spiritually a Buddhist. I didn't know that until Jim died. But the more I read and thought, the more I realized it is the system of belief which is the most compatible with me. In case you don't know, that's odd, coming from a forty-nine-year-old, formerly Baptist, West Texan female with a deacon father.

The truth is, to me enlightenment seems a far more desirable and human concept than salvation. To put it metaphorically, I am less interested in basking in the light of another's glory than I am in having the light enter me and become me. It requires a different attitude than the one I grew up with, but I find I'm a lot more comfortable with the new attitude than I was with the old one. I guess I'm used to working for what I get. And, believe me, it has been work. I still have more questions than answers when it comes to my personal odyssey.

As I was preparing this speech, I remembered that I'd written some things about Buddhism in a journal I kept after Jim died. I'd like to share those words with you now, because they have an immediacy and a freshness my words now lack. I wrote this particular entry on December 30, 1984, six weeks and two days after his death:

I find so much in Buddhism alluring. What sticks for me is what I suppose sticks for most Westerners—the idea of giving up the Self—its endless fascinations, permutations, gyrations, machinations—so much the subject and object of study. So many paeans to passion—"A man's reach should exceed his grasp—or what's a Heaven for?" Nations of meat-eaters from which I am derived. Aspiration, consummation, ambition. The power and the glory forever—Amen. Competition, capitalism, industry.

Tranquility so scarce, passivity so misconstrued. How do I fold into myself and unfold to the universe? Can I strive to cease striving?

Acceptance. Of what is and what is not? How do I let go of my "figuring out"? And do I really want to?

How can I think of nothing without thinking of Nothing?

Who will care in a hundred years what I am suffering now? And if the answer is "no one," then should I cease to suffer? Can I? Can I choose to cease to suffer and yet live? I don't know. I only know that I alone can make that choice—if there is such a choice to be made.

Jim is gone. Someday I will be gone. Will any of our suffering count? Is it counting now? Or is suffering not the coin?

Reincarnation is another attractive idea. I wish I believed in it. It would be such a blessing to see this as part of a progression—to believe that my soul is linked with Jim's and that we have aeons in which to perfect ourselves—time after time to cross each other's path, to show one another greater and greater compassion until we no longer wrestle with love and mortality and who belongs to whom.

This past December, I spent a weekend watching a Joseph Campbell series called "Transformations of Myth Through Time." His lecture on Buddhism was naturally the most relevant to me, and Campbell reminded me that there are aspects I find virtually impossible to master— what he stated was the essence of Buddha consciousness—"joyful participation in the sorrows of the world." That kind of letting go, of not simply resigning to a sometimes very hard fate, but embracing it as the one which, as someone put it, "permits of no substitution"—I'll admit that ideal lies beyond my capability much of the time. It strikes me though as the ultimate sanity, the most correct understanding of the great what-it-is and what-I-am.

I both laughed and backed up the tape several times to hear Campbell say, "If you're falling, dive." Is that perfect or what? Do the thing which has to be done. However it goes, be in it, participate fully.

Not to insult those of you even more familiar with it than I, but the short form of Buddha's message is, "Right action precedes right thought. Right thought precedes right being." Right action—overcome by the sorrows of the world, by death and pain and suffering, Buddha sits. By sitting, he stills himself and engages his mind in contemplation—right thought. When actions and thoughts are correct, he contacts that which is universal, which contains no opposites and enables him to rise above desire and fear—thus achieving right being.

When I watched the Campbell series, I was in something of a personal crisis and so I took Buddha's example and forced myself to sit. The longer I sat, the more I realized that, although my every action was understandable, given my vulnerabilities and history, my actions weren't the correct ones because they were driven by fear and desire. The things I desired are eminently comprehensible (aren't most desirable things, like being loved and having my son back?), but they had the drawback of not necessarily being the things that were available at the time and in the way I wanted them. A significant portion of all desire is ego (in the lay sense). Consequently, it pays to examine it carefully—and when I have, I've always found it's lousy with me, me, me, me, me. It has brought me up short more than once to realize that much of the grief in my life has really been a presentable facade for what's essentially my wounded narcissism. I shouldn't lose anything. I'm too special.

Anyway, I accept the wisdom of, "If you're falling, dive." Maybe that's because I've fallen time and again in various ways and survived it. Maybe that's because, as a suicide survivor, I know that one of the most devastating things about suicide is the survivor's sense of losing control, and diving during a fall is about not simply accepting but participating and taking back a portion of control. Maybe it's a sense of the mystic Campbell talked about— the undergirding and universal consciousness which is our source and our destination. Believing in that, I achieve a certain equanimity that is impossible without it.

In both my recent crisis and my suicide survivorship, I have been guided by Buddhist principles. I believe I've taken the correct action, letting go of my fear and desire and diving. This led to correct thought, which was that I can only live the life I've been given. And finally, it led to correct being, which means that, whatever befalls me, I possess Buddha consciousness and, in the deepest sense, I am complete. I know The Way because it's where I came from and where I'm bound. That's not dependent on my losses being restored to me. It's simply acceptance, pure acceptance of all that is and was and will be. Joyful participation in the sorrows of the world.

What comes our way must be embraced and integrated. We must be willing to be, as Rilke put it, "The crystal cup that shattered even as it rang" because, to experience the infinite source of our own most intense vibration, we have to accept shattering and dissolving.

We have to dive as we're falling.

It's the only way to fly.

# SIXTEEN

# Strong Love

I BELIEVE THAT ONLY LOVE survives and heals, only love is stronger than death.

We have within us a dynamic balance, what Freud called Eros and Thanatos. He drew the names from Greek mythology—Eros, or Cupid, is the god of love and Thanatos is Death personified. The concepts are not as simple as all that and Freud wrote a lot on the subject, constructing an elaborate mosaic of ideas. However, the gist of it is that within each of us there is an impulse to love, to grow, to be strong, and a co-equal desire to hate, to die, and to dissolve. Most of the time we repress this second half of our personal equation. Obviously, the suicide doesn't.

What sometimes gets lost in a consideration of Eros is its self-containment. We tend to think of love in terms of what we give others, rather than what we give ourselves. I said it this way once, "Our souls cry out for something or someone to abide with us—and who is there to tell us to look to simple friendship and the ultimate knowledge that we abide with ourselves? How would we hear such a homely, small voice in the bombast? We love the big LOVE of slogans—and the bigger the better. Love is all we need! Love conquers all! And, that quiet love that starts with ourselves and maintains ourselves and blesses ourselves; that love that never deserts us because it *is* us; *that* love often goes begging."*

And, in a slightly different vein, "What's more complicated than the human heart? We want the most elusive things, clutching at approximations which we then reject, never understanding that perfect love and inner peace are only realized by loving others less than perfectly (but at every opportunity) and making ourselves peaceful people."

Now there's a task—making yourself peaceful. But I would maintain that, if you pull it off, you are living that self-love, that Eros that Freud was talking about.

I'm not especially good at loving myself. I've worked on it for years, but I didn't have an auspicious beginning. I understand that lots of people don't, and they're the ones I want to reach. I want to say to them, "Hold on. Keep trying. You don't have to be the best, you just need to tell yourself you're good enough."

I think of how many ways and how many times I said that to Jim. I don't mean to tell you I got it all right because I certainly didn't. I was impatient a lot of the time and downright abusive when he was small (though I didn't see it that way at the time, having been abused myself). I had the usual parental stake in my child doing well and reflecting well on me. But I know I said positive things to him—and I know how often he deflected me. I'd say I don't understand it, but I partially do. My own self-esteem is built on what I've accomplished, what I can do. It isn't autonomous; it doesn't come from within but from the accumulation of goals met and good jobs done. It also comes from having learned to love and admire certain things about myself, and an intrinsic part of that has been allowing others to love and admire me. That's where Jim and I differed—and I don't understand why I could accept those things and he couldn't.

*Sue Chance, "Loss and Resolution," *Journal of Poetry Therapy* 2, no. 2 (Winter 1988).

I remember being taken aback with the idea that, if we try to live in splendid isolation, never taking anything from those who offer, we are being selfish. I must have stumbled across that in my early twenties because I've acted on it ever since. And I've seen it borne out time and again. I remember startling a young man who was interviewing me for a local paper. He mentioned that he'd ended a long-term relationship and, as he put it, "Inflicted my pain and suffering on my friends for several months." I told him he might look at that differently, saying, "What you really did was offer your friends an opportunity to help you—and what could be a more flattering testimonial to their importance to you and your confidence in them?"

I'm not saying we have a right to dump on our friends continually or to expect them to do therapy on us when they lack the necessary equipment and credentials. A lot of times, troubled people use their long-suffering friends to avoid seeing a therapist and "taking the cure" (which often entails no small amount of discomfort). The current term for those who keep accepting what the chronic complainers dish out is "co-dependent," and you can get help for that.

What I am saying is that we are inextricably linked with those around us and that those linkages carry an obligation to both give and receive. To constantly deflect the proffered gifts of others is, at minimum, ungracious and, at maximum (as in Jim's case), lethal.

Shortly after he died, there was a popular song David mentioned once when he called. He said he couldn't sit through it and I knew exactly what he meant, since it had the same effect on me. We both identified the song with Jim because in it the singer communicates that he's barely hanging on and that he needs this new person to show him love so he'll have something to believe in. I guess I'd still have the same gut reaction and be upset if I heard the song today. However, after I looked at our home movies on the first of Jim's birthdays to roll around after he died, I wrote the following entry:

**7–18–85**   I'm giving thanks today. It would have been Jim's 26th birthday, and it's raining. I'd like to thank God, Nature, Coincidence for providing the rain—I appreciate it. Who would want a pretty day?

The last few weeks have been worse, the clouds amassing. Today is, in some sense, a relief. There is the hope of rain and tears—that, out of something drear comes something new—or nourishment of something old perhaps.

My sister was the taker of home movies, and she had them all put on a videotape. I got it last week. There was my fourteen-year-old self, playing with my baby niece. There was my pregnant sixteen-year-old self. There was Jim. A baby on my lap, a toddler throwing kisses with great care, a small maniac on a swing, a wagon puller, a puppy player-with. And as I watched, I saw the matrix in which Jim was embedded. I saw a family, so very imperfect, who loved in all the silent and boisterous ways most families love—"the family usages" Whitman talked about, the coalitions. I held myself and asked of the blank ceiling, sky, universe, *"Why?"* When love is so apparent, when love is so real?

And I seem to see, in a glimmering only, that all of my answers are not really answers at all. Jim's suicide was not an equality—the sides of the equation don't balance. I don't know the mathematics of irrationality, but I do know the result was greater than the sum of its parts. What we did or failed to do were not the building blocks of this edifice. Jim, himself, was constructed with more care than most, even though the principal builders were amateurs. Jim did what he did in an agony of self-doubt, amplified apparently by alcohol. A right-handed person, he used his left hand to end his life, and the symbolism says it all.

I will always miss him and love him. And, as I said the day after his death, I will always feel I failed him. No amount of persuasion or reason can change that because I alone know all the ways in which I did. But we all fail, don't we? Who can love in a perfect way?

I had a son. His name was Jim. His name was Love. His name was me.

# SEVENTEEN

# A Survivor's Benediction

SEVERAL TIMES I'VE BEEN ASKED to talk with mental health professionals about working with survivors. I think the most important thing I tell them is to validate the survivor's anger. It's so easy to see the guilt—they come in rending their garments with it. But anger is *so* much tougher to experience when its object is dead. As I said in my address to the Menninger alumni:

> Survivors suffer the double despair of bereavement and impotence. They are powerless to alter what has happened to them, and they are justifiably angry at the deceased for having put them through a devastating experience. They feel shame, yet a part of them rebels against being ashamed of what someone else did without consulting them. They have been cast in the role of murderers when, in truth, they are victims. For persons who commit suicide have committed secret murder; they have killed themselves rather than their intended victims.
>
> Survivors perceive such thoughts as irrational. They believe that to be so enraged, so ashamed, so resentful is unjustified. After all, the deceased paid the ultimate price for their troubled relationships. How can the survivors complain? It takes time and help to accept the rational

basis of their thoughts, and to the extent that they do so, they find order amidst the chaos.*

Men characteristically do a better job with anger than women do, and hardly anyone does a worse job than a bereaved mother. As a bereaved father put it recently in a letter to me about his daughter's death, "All of my cells oppose this reality." How much more true is that of a mother, whose every cell was involved in the creation of her child's life? Our children issue from our bodies and they are always more ours than they are their father's. When that child dies, what death, short of our own, takes more?

How difficult it is, then, to experience anger at that version of ourselves. Every instinct says we are to nurture and protect our offspring—and the inclination is go on doing that ad infinitum. Hasn't everybody known a bereaved mother who erected either a physical or emotional shrine to a child so idealized as to be unrecognizable to the people who knew him or her?

Well, I'd leave that alone if it weren't for the fact that it's a killer. If that mother has other children, they can't help but suffer by comparison to their now perfect sibling. And if, like me, she has no more children, she is guaranteed to wallow in guilt for as long as she goes on distorting reality. Because if you maintain that your child was flawless, then death by his own hand automatically becomes your responsibility.

I remember my astonishment when I heard Edwin Shneidman say at the 1987 American Association of Suicidology meeting that suicide is consistent with the rest of the suicide's life. Those who commit suicide typically didn't handle past disturbances well, have a very limited capacity to endure psychological pain, and have a penchant for constriction (a kind of narrowed perspective), black-and-white thinking, and running from their problems.

Fits Jim to a tee.

*Sue Chance, "Surviving Suicide: A Journey to Resolution," *Bulletin of the Menninger Clinic* 52, no. 1 (January 1988).

Does it pain me to admit that? Yes, it does. But it would pain me more to go on believing that his choice was driven by *my* mistakes and shortcomings. The questions are not, What did I do wrong and what should I have done differently? They are, Why did he persist in things that didn't work and why would he not go for help or accept it when it was offered? Those questions are unanswerable, of course, but then so were the original ones. The ones about him are simply more to the point.

Needless to say, I got very, very angry at Jim. I was in a towering rage the whole third year of my bereavement. But gradually a tempering process set in as I realized more and more that, in an ironic way, Jim was considerate. He spared even those he was angriest at from finding his body: and that is a *major* trauma to survivors. I can only imagine the horror of seeing the mutilated body of someone you love. I listened to Mariette Hartley describe the suicide of her father in the next room and watched as she gestured helplessly, saying, "And, I cleaned my father's"—she was too overcome for a moment to continue, but we all filled in the blanks, knowing the unspoken words were—"brains off the wall."

I amplified my agony at first, visualizing that moment and its immediate consequences. My medical training was a kind of curse, since I could very adequately imagine that through-and-through explosion of his beloved head. However, I soon realized that persisting in those images was a sure path to madness, and when I caught myself doing it, I'd scold myself, saying, "Just knock it the hell off, Sue." Believe it or not, that was effective. Incidentally, there is a name for that technique—it's called thought-stopping and it's exactly what it sounds like. By hook or by crook, you make yourself change the subject. Most survivors could stand to do it more often.

You have to go by way of anger. It's intrinsic to the survival process. Only by doing it can you begin to experience forgiveness—of the suicide and of yourself. It's like one of those monsters of the mind that's always gaining on you in your dreams. You have to face it if you're ever going to stop running.

I want to remind you of something I said early in this book: you don't know what anybody else is feeling unless he or she tells you. We often take suicide as a punishment, but I'm here to tell you I don't think that's a major portion of its intent. In fact, I think sometimes it's totally inapplicable. The thing I've come to realize is that I can't understand Jim's pain any more than he could have predicted mine. I don't know what I meant to him. He didn't know what he meant to me. Even those closest to us remain an enigma in many ways.

I also believe that, whatever the failures of a parent or parents, at some point in time the individual takes over his or her own destiny. In working with adolescents from very sick families, I finally decided that the best thing I could do is give them the following lecture: "You want to tell me how much your parents have messed up and how much pain they've caused you. I believe you. I know that your complaints are legitimate. But you're coming closer and closer to the time in your life when you can take over and make it better for yourself. That's going to be your choice: whether you stay stuck in blaming and moaning about all the things which have been unfair or get on with it and do the best you can with what you have."

Kids don't like that message any better than adults do, any better than I did the first time I gave it to myself. But it has the utility of being both true and ultimately helpful.

I do not like my parents and I do not like the things they did to me. However, I am responsible for who I am now. There is no way I can reasonably say that, at forty-nine, I am more a product of the first fifteen years spent with them than I am of the past thirty-four years spent with myself. I would, in fact, be very ashamed of myself if it were true.

We are all a work in progress. Life isn't about getting everything right. It's about adapting, about learning to love the sorrows of our changing faces. Suicide short-circuits that. It is not only an untimely end but a failure of adaptation and growth. As Shakespeare said in *Othello,* "How poor are they that have not patience!/What wound did ever heal but by degrees?"

The suicide doesn't wait around for that healing. His survivors have to believe it's coming or they will commit suicide themselves. And there are myriad ways to do that—drugs and alcohol, emotional isolation, living in a fantasy, to name a few. If, on the other hand, they want to live and heal, they have to acknowledge that it is the suicide who bears the ultimate responsibility. Accepting this enables them to pick up the threads of their own lives and relationships and go on with them.

There have been changes in how I view death and changes in how I view life. Much remains a mystery, but I know more about loss and resolution than most people. I know how to survive. I know how to be strong. I know how to love.

Near the end of my journal, I said some words of appreciation about my little cat. Then I said:

> My cat has joined the procession of family, friends, teachers, patients, poets, and writers who have helped me get on with my life. For I have to get on with my life. It's an obligation I owe to myself, an obligation I owe to Jim. He rejected his life, but I can't. I must use his life to master my own. And perhaps that mastery will be a form of creation.

Mastering and creating ourselves is a lifelong task. In order to do it, we must hold fast to that enduring, abiding love that embodies the universal good. Our love for others and for ourselves comes from and returns to that source.

That source is where my son has gone.

And I believe that source is stronger than death.

# Resources

To FIND OUT if there's a survivors group near you, call your local library, Mental Health Association, or crisis center, or contact:

> The American Suicide Foundation
> 1045 Park Avenue
> New York, NY 10028
> (800) 531-4477

> or

> The American Association of Suicidology
> 2459 South Ash
> Denver, CO 80222
> (303) 692–0985

The latter group publishes a quarterly newsletter called *Surviving Suicide,* which is helpful for those who don't feel up to a group.

For information on Compassionate Friends, the organization for bereaved parents (but which is also attended by siblings, grandparents, etc.), call the same agencies above, or write.

> Compassionate Friends
> P.O. Box 1347
> Oak Brook, IL 60521
> (312) 323–5010

# A Note on Symptoms

SURVIVORS OFTEN SUFFER FROM several psychiatric syndromes, including depression, post-traumatic stress disorder, and physical complaints which have a psychological basis. To educate the reader further, I have listed the diagnostic "criteria" a psychiatrist uses to determine whether one of these is present, based on the American Psychiatric Association's *Diagnostic and Statistical Manual, Third Edition, Revised (DSM-III-R).* If you meet these criteria, I'd strongly urge you to consider seeking psychiatric care, as medications are available which may afford you tremendous relief.

## MAJOR DEPRESSION

A. Loss of interest or pleasure in usual activities. A mood described as sad, blue, hopeless, low, down in the dumps, irritable. This mood must be prominent and fairly persistent.

B. At least four of the following symptoms nearly every day for at least two weeks:
  1. Either poor or increased appetite with either significant weight loss (without dieting) or significant weight gain.
  2. Either not sleeping well or sleeping excessively.

3. Restlessness or lethargy.
4. Loss of interest or pleasure in usual activities or a decrease in sexual drive.
5. Loss of energy; fatigue.
6. Feelings of worthlessness, self-reproach, or excessive or inappropriate guilt.
7. Poor concentration, slowed thinking, and indecisiveness.
8. Recurrent thoughts of death, suicidal ideas, or attempts.

## POST-TRAUMATIC STRESS DISORDER

A. Existence of an event or circumstance which would cause distress in almost anyone.

B. Reexperiencing of the trauma one of the following ways:
1. Recurrent recollections of the event (often despite efforts not to remember).
2. Recurrent dreams of the event.
3. Suddenly acting or feeling as if the traumatic event were happening again.

C. Decreased responsiveness and/or involvement with the external world, beginning after the trauma and shown by one of the following:
1. Markedly decreased interest in one or more significant activities.
2. Feeling of detachment or distance from others.
3. Constricted affect (diminished ability to show a full range of feelings).

D. At least two of the following symptoms that were not present before the trauma:
1. Excessive alertness; easily startled.
2. Sleep disturbance.
3. Guilt about surviving when others have not, or about the behavior required for survival.
4. Memory impairment or trouble concentrating.
5. Avoidance of activities which arouse recollection of the traumatic event.

6. Intensification of symptoms when exposed to anything which reminds one of the traumatic event.

## PSYCHOLOGICAL FACTORS AFFECTING PHYSICAL CONDITION

A. Something psychologically meaningful occurred around the same
time the patient developed a physical condition or the event caused a
worsening of a pre-existing physical condition.

B. The physical condition has either physical findings (e.g., rheumatoid
arthritis) or occurs in a medically predictable way (e.g., migraine
headache, vomiting).

# Bibliography

Auden, W. H. Foreword to *Markings,* by Dag Hammarskjold. New
    York: Knopf, 1980.
*Buddhist Scriptures.* Selected and translated by Edward Conze. Har-
    mondsworth: Penguin Books, 1959.
Campbell, Joseph. *Transformations of Myth Through Time.* New York:
    Harper & Row, 1990.
Chance, Sue. "Doctors and Bereaved Parents." *Resident and Staff
    Physician* 33, no. 7 (June 1987): 135–137.
———. "God, Patients, and Psychiatrists." *Psychiatric Annals* 18, no. 7
    (July 1988): 432–435.
———. "Loss and Resolution." *Journal of Poetry Therapy* 2, no. 2
    (Winter 1988): 93–98.
———. "Surviving Suicide: A Journal to Resolution." *Bulletin of the
    Menninger Clinic* 52, no. 1 (January 1988): 30–39.
Franz, Marie-Louise von. *On Dreams and Death.* Boston: Shambhala
    Productions, 1986.
Freud, E. L., ed. *Letters of Sigmund Freud.* New York: Basic Books,
    1961.
Freud, Sigmund. *Jokes and Their Relation to the Unconscious.* New
    York: Norton, 1960.
Kushner, Harold. *When Bad Things Happen to Good People.* New
    York: Avon Books, 1981.
LeGuin, Ursula. *Always Coming Home.* New York: Bantam Books,
    1986.

Lewis, C. S. *A Grief Observed.* New York: Seabury Press, 1961.

Lukas, Christopher, and Henry M. Seiden. *Silent Grief: Living in the Wake of Suicide.* New York: Scribners, 1987.

Menninger, Karl. "Hope." Address before the 115th Annual Meeting of the American Psychiatric Association, 1959.

———. *Love Against Hate.* New York: Harvest Books, 1970. (Originally published 1942.)

Shneidman, Edwin. *Definition of Suicide.* New York: Wiley, 1985.

Simonton, Karl and Stephanie, and James Creighton. *Getting Well Again.* New York: St. Martin's Press, 1978.

Twain, Mark. *Letters from the Earth.* Greenwich, Conn.: Fawcett Crest, 1967. (Originally published 1938.)

# Index

*Index*